Hope for the
Praying Nation

Destiny Image Books by Don Nori Sr.

The Voice
Supernatural Destiny
Romancing the Divine
Manifest Presence
Breaking Generational Curses
Secrets of the Most Holy Place
Secrets of the Most Holy Place Volume 2
Tales of Brokenness
The Angel and the Judgement
You Can Pray in Tongues
The Prayer God Loves to Answer
Breaking Demonic Strongholds
So You Want to Change the World?
How to Find God's Love
God: Out of Control, Out of the Box, Out of Time
No More Sour Grapes
The Love Shack
The Hope of the Nation That Prays
The God Watchers
Morning Prayer
God
The Forgotten Mountain

HOPE
for the Praying
NATION

PETITIONING HEAVEN
for Change in Your Country

Don Nori Sr.

Previously published 2001, The Power of a Praying Nation by Treasure House, an Imprint of Destiny Image® Publishers, Inc. ISBN 0-7684-3045-3

DESTINY IMAGE® PUBLISHERS, INC.
PO Box 310, Shippensburg, PA 17257-0310
"Promoting Inspired Lives"

Cover design by Eileen Rockwell
This book and all other Destiny Image and Destiny Image Fiction books available at Christian bookstores and distributors worldwide.
For more information on foreign distributors, call 717-532-3040.
Or reach us on the Internet: www.destinyimage.com

ISBN 13 TP: 978-0-7684-0971-0
ISBN 13 Ebook: 978-0-7684-0972-7
ISBN 13 Hardcover: 978-0-7684-4693-7
ISBN 13 Large Print: 978-0-7684-4694-4

For Worldwide Distribution, Printed in the U.S.A.
1 2 3 4 5 6 / 19 18 17 16

Contents

Section I

A Call to Prayer

God Is Listening

God loves to hear our prayers. More importantly, He loves to answer our prayers. Contrary to popular belief, He is intimately involved with our lives. He sees, hears, protects, and provides for us. He also teaches, leads, and opens doors for us that we could never open for ourselves. In short, He is lovingly involved in our lives wherever and whenever we allow Him to be. He does not need to be convinced, bribed, or otherwise begged to respond to us. He is God. We are His creation. His love, compassion, and mercy toward humankind is far greater than any human could imagine, and He is already determined to bring humanity into a place of peace with Him—and harmony with each other. We need only to knock on heaven's door in humility and faith to experience the love and power of God before our eyes.

We have more of a role to play in prayer than we have understood. The love of God permeates everything we are—body, soul, and spirit. Our lives are intertwined with His in remarkable ways. God is interested in a monologue. He is not waiting for our "honey-do" list. He loves His creation and wants personal fellowship with humanity. He is dynamically connected with us in real time. Those who wait to listen and yield to Him discover His life, His plan, and our part in it.

For we are not just random beings left here on this planet to fend for ourselves. We are not tiny cells that have per chance collided and have become living, thinking souls. We are not on just on a planet whirling through space to an indeterminate destination. We have been purposefully designed, specifically crafted, and lovingly woven in the womb of our mothers. We are not afterthoughts of God. We are the center of His attention, just as we are the center of activity of those who love us. God is thoughtfully, intricately involved within a sentient species that barely acknowledges His existence. Yet He continues patiently, lovingly, calling us to Himself; wooing us, as it were, to His unfailing love and never-ending compassionate mercy.

Every time I bow my heart before our Lord, I am certain of His desire to bring wholeness to my life and family. I am convinced that He always has our best interest before Him. It is God's single-minded desire for my well-being that gives me the rest and confidence I have to keep going forward in everyday life. I am leaning on Him. I am convinced that He takes up my lack to do supernaturally what I cannot do in my own strength.

And here is the good news for you. I am not special. He does not love me more or less than He loves anyone else. The things He has done for me He will do for everyone who calls on Him in sincere desire and humility. We are all the same. We are all looking for the best that life has to give us. The best is found in our Lord. Those who pray will understand what I am saying and will, sometimes to their surprise, see the hand of God in their lives in a way that is absolutely amazing.

As the Bible says, *"It is the Father's good pleasure to give you the Kingdom"* (Luke 12:32). God did not make it complicated. He did not make it difficult. He wants us to experience, to live every day in the fullness of joy, peace, and inner contentment. If we do not know this, it is difficult, if not impossible, to believe that He will respond to our prayer. He does not have to be convinced to love us, care for us, protect us. He is fully focused on His creation—you and me.

He is fully committed to us and the dream He has placed within us. From the moment of our conception, God gave us not only our unique physical DNA, He also placed within us our spiritual DNA. That spiritual DNA is the dream, the destiny, the contribution we are intended to give to this planet. Having done that, He is fully engaged, on our behalf, to bring it to pass. This is our confidence, this is our assurance, if we ask Him anything that will aid the dream He has placed within us, He will do it.

The Winning Formula

No, there is not a formula in the traditional sense, but there is definitely a pattern that aligns us with Him that assures His will can be done in the shortest amount of time. The formula for being certain we experience answers to our prayers is simple, clear, and precise. The formula is not a strict set of words to say, nor is it found in repeating prayers that someone has written. Prayer is a relational, trustworthy, and very warm conversation with God. He loves to hear us talk to Him. He loves it when we are able to tell Him our fears, our pain, our struggles. But He also loves it when we tell Him our joys, our hopes, and our dreams for the future.

> *Prayer is a relational, trustworthy,*
> *and very warm conversation*
> *with God.*

Authentic prayer is spontaneous conversation. It is the way we talk to people every day. Words merely express the emotion we feel. They form the hopes we have in thought that others can clearly understand, appreciate, and respond to. Spontaneous conversation between friends is most exciting, encouraging, fruitful, and honest. It engenders mutual trust, confidence, and hope. To be sure, God does not need to be instructed, counseled, or directed as how best to answer our prayers. Nonetheless, inner honesty is the foundation to real relationship and in turn, answered prayer.

Many years ago when Cathy and I were nearing our wedding day, a well-meaning friend gave me a small book to read that he said would prepare me for our first few weeks together as husband and wife. I was grateful. A twenty-year-old has little wisdom when it comes to such things. I was eager for the help. But when I got to "The Wedding Night" chapter, I realized that some things are best left to spontaneity.

No, I was not going to memorize several paragraphs to lovingly recite to my new wife as we entered our hotel room. I was not going mechanically list the things this author was certain would "break the ice," reduce the tension. I imagined taking my new wife into my arms and holding that little book behind her where she could not see it. Then with tenderness and love, I would read things to her most tender and intimate. Ridiculous, right? Yes, there are some things best left to the spontaneous conversation of the moment. In fact, when we are talking about answered prayer, authentic communication is the way to go.

The winning formula is about attitude more than anything else. The condition of your heart will either help or hinder God's ability to answer your prayers. When we understand our part in our prayer life, we will see the supernatural activity of God at every turn. There are three simple ways to be sure we are in the right frame of mind when we pray:

1. Live in a genuine attitude of forgiveness to all people. A cursory and honest review of our own lives will certainly show us that we too have issues for which we need forgiveness, both before God and others around. Living in an attitude of forgiveness settles our heart and keeps us in a positive frame of mind as we pray.

2. Remember who you are without the grace of God. Humility before God and others keeps us below the radar of the enemy and those who would want to harm us. Humility is the result of searching our hearts and allowing the Holy Spirit to gently nudge us back to the place of softness toward God. It assures that our faith is sufficient and His love for us complete in every way. Humility disarms the battles that want to rage against those who have done us harm. It keeps our hearts open and trusting, thus making prayer easier and our confidence for answered prayer high.

3. A willing heart will open the heavens on your behalf. Just as prayer is not a monologue to God, the answer is not completely God-dependent. Often, the very solution to prayer is within the ability and reach of the one praying. God will often answer our prayer through personal instruction and direction. Staying in an attentive attitude as you pray will not only give you confidence and assurance that He hears you, but He may also be speaking the answer to you as you pray. If you don't know to be listening, you may not hear Him.

Reformation Begins with Me

Sometimes I wonder what we expect God to do specifically when we pray for national repentance and revival. Who will be the first to repent? Who is the first to be convicted? Does a nation repent from the top down or does it begin with each individual? If it begins with the individual, who will be the first to respond to God? It seems to me the answer is much simpler than we have thought. If want to start a fire, I am the one who strikes the match. I am the one who initially takes the step to ignite a fire that can sweep the land. For no matter how right I think I am, I am not thereby excused. If I want revival for the nation, I will allow God to search my heart first and foremost as I refuse to be a hindrance to the very prayer I want God to answer.

Therefore I assume nothing. I do not consider myself good just because I go to church and do everything I think I should be doing. No, I know that the depth of humankind's depravity is hidden by the religious attitude of outward conformation to a given set of moral boundaries and Christian precepts. But if I am as serious as I think I am about turning a nation to God, I will begin turning the nation by turning myself Godward and asking the Holy Spirit to search me.

> *Search me, O God, and know my heart; try me and know my anxieties; and see if there is any wicked way in me, and lead me in the way everlasting* (Psalm 139:23-24).

> *Behold, You desire truth in the inward parts, and in the hidden part You will make me to know wisdom. Purge me with*

hyssop, and I shall be clean; wash me, and I shall be whiter than snow (Psalm 51:6-7).

As one who absolutely loves prayer and fellowship with my Lord, I live in an attitude of these verses in Psalms 139 and 51. I have a lifestyle of broken repentance. Some think the concept is an oxymoron. But that is only because those who think that way do not know the joy and contentment of a clear conscience before God and others.

Broken repentance is not depressing, it is uplifting, exhilarating, strengthening. It keeps the mind free to explore the wonders of now, instead of rehashing the mistakes of the past. Regret over past failures drains strength, sidetracks destiny, and causes us to shrink away from the only One who can free us from such torment. It makes no sense. Even the most committed to the Lord will fail in one way or another from time to time. Sometimes more often than one would like to admit. To allow the Holy Spirit unlimited access to our hearts with His unbiased searchlight is the surest way to daily peace and unfettered hope for the future, beginning with your own.

Wholeness

We are not children who need to be pampered. To be sure, we need to be children in our fresh and childlike trust in our Lord. But wholeness belongs to the open-hearted, the humble, the teachable. Wholeness belongs to those who are not afraid to admit that they are not presently whole. This is not a degrading or disqualifying attitude. It is quite the opposite. For it reminds us who we are apart from His grace. Preserving this heart condition of broken repentance keeps us soft toward others, open to opposing views, correction, and redirection. None of us are an island unto ourselves. Without the ability to hear what we do not want to hear for one reason or another will ultimately cause us to miss the mark of God's primary dream for our lives.

Wholeness depends upon our willingness to have a course correction in attitude, doctrine, politics, relationships, and many more than can be listed here. Let's determine in our hearts today that we will be children in our faith and hope in our Lord. But let us also determine that we will be mature in matters of our own growth and spiritual development.

Hope Springs from the Heart

If my heart was not overflowing with hope, I would not have written this book. If my heart was not confident in the power of God toward humanity, there would be no reason to write, no reason to believe for better days and no reason to pray at all. But the truth is, God is not a God of judgment. He is not a God of wrath. All of His judgment, all of His wrath was nailed to the cross of Christ. The consequences of sin and rebellion should never be mistaken for God's wrath. We bring that upon ourselves with life-styles that are naturally opposed to what is best for our body and soul. We do not need God's wrath as we do a great job all by ourselves in bringing to this planet the consequences of our rebellious living.

Our God is full of forgiving love, compassionate power, and never-ending mercy. No, God is not a God of judgment. There is nothing He wants more than for humanity to come to Him, to love Him, to allow Him to show them the awesome plan He has for each individual person. To that end, God waits for our prayers, for our permission for Him to take control of our lives and circumstance. He is ready to teach us, direct us, fill us with wisdom, confidence, and peace. When we pray in broken repentance, giving Him open access to our lives, things change dramatically around us, beginning within our own hearts.

CHAPTER 1

A Praying Nation Is…

Blessed is the nation whose God is the Lord…
(Psalm 33:12).

A Praying Nation Is a Powerful Nation

A praying nation has confidence and assurance that is unparalleled among the world's community of states. Often misunderstood as arrogance, this power is proven divine by her generosity and humility toward the rest of the world. Her power does not rest in her armies or in her military hardware. Her power is not measured by her economic accomplishments or her technological advances. Her power rests in her people, their sincere, authentic prayers, and in the One to whom she prays.

In quiet confidence and assurance, her hidden strength is in an all-powerful God who they serve with godly fear. They have to understand their ways may not be His ways, their ideas may not be His. They have lived long enough to experience life apart from His will. Now they have learned. Prayer with humble hearts and open minds is the key that will preserve their nation in an atmosphere of growth, opportunity, and fulfillment.

God will bless and protect a broken, repentant nation. Of course, a nation is the sum of the people who make up that nation. Indeed, without its people, there is no nation at all. When the people are repentant, the nation is repentant. When her people fear God, the nation fears God. It matters not who in leadership believes or does not believe. God wants us to believe and He will, without question, take care of the rest. Those who pray bring about change. Those who listen to Him will be engaged in the process of change from within. This is the secret of a nation's power. There is no question about it. A repentant and praying nation is a powerful nation.

A Praying Nation Is a Loving Nation

Our national security was woven into the very fabric of who we are as a people. In spite of how some would attempt to rewrite our history, our founders established this country on the eternal principles of prayer and faith toward God. Had security not been established at our beginnings, it would be as illusive as it is to so many nations today. No, we cannot make this a secure nation—we can only protect and preserve the security that is a foundational building block of our history. Such security is not based in words but in confidence in God Himself.

Our nation is protected because God protects repentant people. His power is much greater than any human words can define, for that would require the ability to understand the greatness of His power to begin with. His reign is above all and carries with it the most formidable resolve that eternity can muster.

Angels hover over a praying nation because of her praying people. They protect her and watch over her children. They are alert and attentive to all her enemies, ready in a moment to protect her from all harm.

The nation that prays has a security that cannot be matched in the universe. There are no armies, no strategies, no plans that can overpower the strength of a praying nation. For her wisdom is born from above, and the courage to carry out that wisdom comes from above.

A praying nation causes Heaven itself to shatter time and space, replacing the vile and the hideous with the purposes of God.

Her edge is her faith in an unseen realm where God alone rules and the affairs of humankind are dictated by a force born of human faith, and heavenly resolve. A praying nation causes Heaven itself to shatter time and space, replacing the vile and the hideous with the purposes of God.

King David ruled over a praying nation. The very existence of that people depended solely upon the relationship between that nation and the God who covered and protected it. King David's Psalm 121 tells us of the understanding and trust he discovered as he prayed to his Lord in the most brutal of circumstances:

I will lift up my eyes to the hills—from whence comes my help? My help comes from the Lord, who made heaven and earth. He will not allow your foot to be moved; He who keeps you will not slumber. Behold, He who keeps Israel shall neither slumber nor sleep. The Lord is your keeper; the Lord is your shade at your right hand. The sun shall not strike you by day, nor the moon by night. The Lord shall preserve you from all evil; He shall preserve your soul. The Lord shall preserve your going out and your coming in from this time forth, and even forevermore.

A Praying Nation Is a Secure Nation

Because a praying nation is loving, she is by nature compassionate and patient. Never mistake her patience and love for weakness, for it is her love that causes her to hope for the impossible and believe the best when there is no basis for it. A bear loves her cubs but is neither weak nor indecisive when it comes to a threat to her offspring. Her love will protect at any cost.

So it is with God and any nation whose people pray. Love causes nations to lay aside the differences with others in the face of human disaster and misery. A loving nation clothes and feeds even her enemies in times of distress. She opposes cruelty and injustice even when it is brought to her foes.

A loving nation exercises patience in all things and does not allow her anger to be kindled easily. But do not mistake her anger for fear, for she is aware of the troubles of the world. She will hope until life itself is threatened, before rising in holy anger and righteous indignation.

A loving nation responds to the needs around her. She cannot turn a deaf ear or a blind eye to suffering of any kind. A praying nation is a loving nation.

A Praying Nation Is a Holy Nation

The praying people of nation understand that their holy words to a holy God are not separate from their unholy actions. They walk softly before their Lord, with reverence, circumspectly allowing the Holy Spirit to search out motives, desires, and lusts. They understand that their primary responsibility is to their own heart, their own actions, hidden desires, and points of thought that run contrary to their Lord. They personally live in broken repentance before their Lord.

Her life is one of quiet repentance, daily confessing her faults as individual citizens and as a nation. She cries to God for mercy and forgiveness, fully confident that whoever repents of sin to the Lord is forgiven. This confessed, corporate sin is summarily cast into the sea of forgetfulness, never to torment the nation again with its blazing guilt and haunting memory.

A praying nation knows that God loves her. She knows His hand is stretched out to her in loving strength and comfort. Her weakness keeps her humble and her love keeps her at His breast in relentless prayer for strength to overcome the sin that seems to befall her so easily.

She is all too aware of her humanity. Her strength is in knowing her weakness; her humility is visible in the cry to the Lord for His strength; her future is in His mercy; her power is in her prayer. A praying nation is a holy nation.

How blessed are the people who live this way! How blessed are the people whose God is the Lord! *"Happy are the people who are in such a state; happy are the people whose God is the Lord!"* (Psalm 144:15).

The praying nation lives in softness and openness to her Lord. She does not presume upon His kindness or demand His attention. A holy nation knows precisely her place in the grand scheme of things and has no desire to change places with Him.

CHAPTER 2

God Loves Us

Why does it seem so hard for us to understand and accept how much God loves us? We were on His mind long before the world came into being. He created us for His pleasure. He gave us His only Son to forgive us and His Holy Spirit to gather us to Himself.

Sometimes it seems we try so hard to figure out the things that are difficult to grasp, that we forget the things that are so simple. God loves us. That is simple. Jesus said it. Look at John 15:9 and 13, *"As the Father has loved Me, so have I loved you...Greater love has no one than this, than to lay down one's life for his friends."*

He cares for us so much more than we can ever imagine. He is constantly with us. In fact, God is so big that He gives His full attention to each one of us individually. That is amazing! He is so big that He focuses on each one of us personally. He knows us intimately. He knows our struggles and our pain. He knows our fears and our sorrows. He knows what holds us back and He knows exactly how to bring us to the heart attitude that can overcome the things that hinder us. God made us with a contribution to this earth and He will not so easily give up on you. He wants you to succeed. He wants you to win. He has already given you everything you need to fulfill what burns in your heart.

Yes, He knows our hopes and our dreams. He knows the deepest desires of our hearts and He knows how all those things work together to make us who we are and to make all our dreams come true. We make it complicated. Or, maybe we allow others to make it complicated for us. But the truth is, you can approach your Lord with confidence. You can be certain that He wants to show you His love in all its vibrant fullness.

There now, it's not so complicated after all. We may not be able to understand ourselves, but there is One who not only understands, but also made us the way we are for a specific purpose.

We are not complicated to God. He loves us personally, totally, passionately. He cares for us and is striving with us to bring all our dreams into reality.

God Loves You

Some people think that the more important you are, the more God will love you. That just is not true. He does not care more for the rich or the famous. He does not love some people more than others. He does not think that some are not worth His love.

God's love is much bigger than your sin and more powerful than your guilt.

He loves us all, no matter what we have done or how far we think we have strayed from Him. His love is much bigger than our sin and more powerful than our guilt. Always remember that God loves who we are. His deepest desire is toward His creation. He will always strive with us, drawing us to Himself. Anytime you think you are far from God, remember this—you are only one short prayer away from His mighty throne within your heart.

The night before He was crucified, Jesus was praying from a hilltop overlooking the city of Jerusalem, the city that was about to crucify Him the next morning. His love was so deep even for those who were about to take His life that He cried out to her inhabitants, "O Jerusalem, Jerusalem, the one who kills the prophets and stones those who are sent to her! *How often I wanted to gather your children together, as a hen gathers her chicks under her wings,* but you were not willing! See! Your house is left to you desolate, for I say to you, you shall see Me no more till you say, *'Blessed is **He** who comes in the name of the Lord!'"*

No, God does not condemn. We go our own way. We make our arrogant plans, and when they fail we blame God for the failure.

But you are not like that. You have experienced His love in ways that only you have known. You know that He gathers. He loves. He fills the repentant heart with good things. His heart is, as it always has been, open to you right now.

God Loves Us!

To try to understand why bad things happen is more than most of us can bear. But we do know that God loves us. This is what we should center our thoughts on, since He is really our only source of comfort. We know that He created us to be just like Him. Long before you were born, God knew you—and knowing you, He loves you. The world can be cruel at times to turn away from us, but we must never forget how much God loves us.

Some people think that they have sinned too much or have ignored Him for too long. They think that God is just like we are. They think He holds grudges and remembers our failures. But God loves us. He is a forgiving God. He is easy to talk to and is anxious to forgive us. All we need to do is ask Him. After all, He loved us so much that He sent His only Son, Jesus, to die in our place. Jesus took all our sins with Him when He went to the cross. When He died, He took all our sins with Him into hell. When He rose from the dead three days later, He left our sins in hell, so they would never be able to make us feel guilty again.

He waits for us to ask Him to forgive us. He waits for us to ask Him to take the sins we have committed and to set us free from the guilt we feel for what we have done.

Oh how deeply God loves us! We must never be afraid of Him. We must never feel that He wants to punish us. The Lord Jesus took our punishment so we could feel God's love and experience the blessings of belonging to Him.

God loves *you* and is waiting for you to come to Him.

CHAPTER 3

God Loves the People of a Nation

I f we are going to ask God to fight for us and protect us, we need to clearly understand that God really does love this land because He loves her people. The truth is, He loves the land because His people live there. He protects the land because He protects us. He is committed to the land because we are on it. His focus is us and our personal and collective well-being: *"For God so loved the world* [us] *that He gave His only begotten Son…"* (John 3:16).

If we are not certain that we are loved, how will we ever have the faith to believe that He will answer our prayers? How will we ever have the courage and assurance to approach Him?

I know God loves this country for several reasons:

1. Her people have fought to maintain a level of peace and an atmosphere of freedom that has allowed the freedom to worship as their own heart dictates. Our freedom allows Christians to share their faith personally and broadcast their faith in whatever medium they choose. As a result of this freedom, the gospel is preached over all media platforms with little governmental interference. We record countless gospel messages and even make movies that preach the gospel. God loves a nation where His people can freely declare their faith and love to Him.

Blessed is the nation whose God is the Lord. The people He has chosen as His own inheritance (Psalm 33:12).

Yes, I know there are threats to that freedom. Those threats have never been so real as they are at this moment in our short history. I also know that there are those who want to silence the gospel. But greater are those who *are with us than are against us*. There are many believers who are called to the marketplace of ideas to challenge the trends and to contend for the presence of God for the people of this nation.

And that is precisely why God is not giving up on this country. It is because He is not giving up on the people who *are* the nation. Today, it is important to know that God loves this nation first and foremost because her people have worked and sacrificed for the freedom of worship and assembly, the freedom of expression and declaration.

2. A generous nation is close to God's heart. Those who have opened their hearts, hands, and wallets to the needs of the world are many. We have compassion and true love for our fellow human beings. We have rebuilt cities after natural disasters and rebuilt nations after wars. Even when the nations who needed help were the nations we had defeated in war, our hearts reached out to them and gave generously. For many years we have joyfully, compassionately, and mercifully been fulfilling the chosen fast that the Lord said was the true fast in Isaiah 58:6-7:

> *Is this not the fast that I have chosen: to loose the bonds of wickedness, to undo the heavy burdens, to let the oppressed go free,*

and that you break every yoke? Is it not the share your bread with the hungry, and that you bring to your house the poor who are cast out; when you see the naked, that you cover him, and not hid yourself from your own flesh?

A nation's generosity makes her a great nation, blessed of the Lord and loved by Him. For God loves a nation that loves the world and is willing to care for it. A godly people see a need and work to come to the rescue as they are compelled by love. Others see need and are restricted by greed and the callous disregard for the human plight.

The generous soul will be made rich, and he that waters will be watered himself (Proverbs 11:25).

The people will curse him who withholds grain, but blessing will be on the head of him who sells it. He who earnestly seeks good find favor, but trouble will come to him who seeks evil. He who trusts in his riches will fall, but the righteous will flourish like foliage (Proverbs 11:26-28).

3. A nation that refuses to stand by idly in the face of oppression around the world is a nation that will live in the favor of God. Others may criticize us for intervention when evil threatens other nations, but God loves us for it. We have put ourselves at risk for the sake of freedom-loving peoples around the world. We have stood against the bullies of the world and fought for the same freedoms that we ourselves have come to cherish.

> *The Lord watches over the strangers; He relieves the fatherless and the widow; but the way of the wicked He turns upside down* (Psalm 146:9).

> *For the Lord loves justice, and does not forsake not His saints; they are preserved forever, but the descendants of the wicked shall be cut off* (Psalm 37:28).

Yes, God loves a nation that will be a light to the nations; an example of true love to the Lord and humankind; an example of selfless giving and compassion to all the needy and destitute of the world. God's nature is revealed when His Son prayed the night before He was crucified—Jesus prayed for Jerusalem (see Matthew 23:37-39). His plan for those who love Him is far from over. It is far from complete. We must not allow ourselves to give in to fear and uncertainty. Rather, let us go before the Lord with confidence and faith. He loves our land, for He loves those who dwell within her borders.

CHAPTER 4

God Wants to Answer Our Prayers

T his may be a new thought to some people, but God really does want to answer our prayers. He does not have to be begged. He does not have to be convinced of our need, for He knows our hearts better than we do. He is not a God who lives somewhere in Heaven and is disinterested in our well-being. He did not create us just to abandon us. He does not leave us as orphans. We are His offspring, His creation, His special treasure.

God wants more than anything else to give us what we ask for. In fact, He wants to give us *more* than we could ask or think or even imagine. He is not merely interested in what we think we need. He also knows what we really need for our own good. And no, that is not just an excuse for why some prayers do not get answered. He is our loving heavenly Father and He knows what is best for us. He knows what we need.

He understands far better than we do what it will take to bring us to the place of deep inner peace and contentment. He answers our prayers according to what He knows will be best for us, not necessarily what we want. He supernaturally cares for us, His moment-by-moment attention to our well-being is far deeper, far more consistent and tangible than we can possibly imagine. Consider this wonderful quote from the Holy Bible:

> *"For My thoughts are not your thoughts, nor are your ways My ways," says the Lord. "For as the heavens are higher than the earth, so are My ways higher than your ways, and My thoughts than your thoughts"* (Isaiah 55:8-9).

This understanding should bring the mature among us much needed assurance of His involvement in our lives. The immature will say that their prayers are not answered because what they prayed for did not come to pass. But consider the whole counsel of God. Consider His love for us, His passion to see our destiny fulfilled to its fullest. One cannot help but to be comforted and encouraged by such knowledge. David had the same sort of struggle at one point in his life. When he realized God's personal attention to his condition, his response was simple, memorable:

> *O Lord, You have searched me and known me. You know my sitting down and my rising up; You understand my thought afar off. You comprehend my path and my lying down, and are acquainted with all my ways. For there is not a word on my tongue, but behold, O Lord, You know it altogether. You have hedged me behind and before, and laid Your hand upon me. Such knowledge is too wonderful for me; it is high, I cannot attain it.*

> *Where can I go from Your Spirit? Or where can I flee from Your presence? If I ascend into heaven, You are there; if I make my bed in hell, behold, You are there. If I take the wings of the morning, and dwell in the*

uttermost parts of the sea, even there Your hand shall lead me, and Your right hand shall hold me. If I say, "Surely the darkness shall fall on me," even the night shall be light about me; indeed, the darkness shall not hide from You, but the night shines as the day; the darkness and the light are both alike to You.

For You formed my inward parts; You covered me in my mother's womb. I will praise You, for I am fearfully and wonderfully made; Marvelous are Your works, and that my soul knows very well. My frame was not hidden from You, when I was made in secret, and skillfully wrought in the lowest parts of the earth. Your eyes saw my substance, being yet unformed. And in Your book they all were written, the days fashioned for me, when as yet there were none of them.

How precious also are Your thoughts to me, O God! How great is the sum of them! If I should count them, they would be more in number than the sand; when I awake, I am still with you (Psalm 139:1-18).

A loving parent gives far more to his children than the child asks. In fact, the child is incapable of even knowing what he really needs. A loving parent's provision for his child is far more complete than a child could ever ask, think or imagine. For the parent has a view of the child's life that the child cannot yet comprehend. Therefore the parent's provision is much greater than the child realizes. It is the same with our heavenly Father. I, for one, am so glad God does not limit His provision to the requests that I ask Him for. I am glad He sees my needs and cares for me according to what He sees I need instead of just what I want.

The Scriptures speak often about how much God wants to answer our prayers. Now we know why He wants to answer them. Our future depends on it. When we quiet our souls and listen, we can know what we should pray for. Then we pray in confidence.

One of my favorite Scripture passages is in the Gospel of Matthew:

> *Ask, and it will be given you; seek, and you will find; knock, and it will be opened to you. For everyone who asks receives, and*

he who seeks finds, and to him who knocks it will be opened. Or what man is there among you, if his son asks for bread, will give him a stone? Or if he asks for a fish, will he give him a serpent? If you then, being evil, know how to give good gifts to your children, how much more will your Father who is in heaven give good things to those who ask Him! (Matthew 7:7-11)

Here are some other wonderful Bible promises from God to think about:

It shall come to pass that before they call, I [God] will answer; and while they are still speaking, I will hear (Isaiah 65:24).

If you abide in Me, and My words abide in you, you will ask what you desire, and it shall be done for you (John 15:7).

So Jesus answered and said to them, "Have faith in God. For assuredly, I say to you, whoever says to this mountain, 'Be removed and be cast into the sea,' and does not doubt in his heart, but believes that those things he says will be done, he will have whatever he says. Therefore I say to you, whatever things you ask when you pray, believe that you receive them, and you will have them (Mark 11:22-24.)

Lord, how they have increased who trouble me! Many are they who rise up against me. Many are they who say of me, "There is no help for him in God." But You, O Lord, are a shield for me, my glory and the One who lifts up my head. I cried to the Lord with my voice, and He heard me from His holy hill. I lay down and slept; I awoke, for the Lord sustained me. I will not be afraid of ten thousands of people who have set themselves against me all around. Arise, O Lord; save me, O my God! For You have struck all my enemies on the cheekbone; You have broken the teeth of the ungodly. Salvation belongs to the Lord. Your blessing is upon Your people.

God Is Good

Our God is a good God. He loves us and wants to care for all our needs because He loves us so completely.

People often feel that God does not care or that He will not answer their prayers because He is too busy with other things. Some people think they are not important enough for the Lord to listen to their needs and their problems.

I have discovered something very important about why we do not believe that He wants to bless us and take care of us. We often feel unworthy because our lives are not what they should be or what they could be. We believe that we have sinned; therefore, God hates us—or at least He will ignore us when we are in need.

Well, nothing is more hopeless than this kind of belief. If we cannot turn to God for help and comfort, who *can* we turn to? He is the most forgiving, the most loving, the most compassionate One in all the universe.

God knows our struggles. He knows our sin. The power of a praying nation begins with the power of individuals praying prayers of genuine repentance. Genuine repentance frees the soul from the guilt and torment of what we have done and sets us securely on the road that pleases God. When we are free from the pain of conviction, our strength can be turned to more positive thought processes. For there is no doubt that there is no more personally brutal force within than than the knowledge of separation from God. Even King David struggled with this when he prayed this powerful prayer:

> *When I kept silent, my bones grew old through my groaning all the day long. For day and night Your hand was heavy upon me; my vitality was turned into the drought of summer. I acknowledged my sin to You, and my iniquity I have not hidden. I said, "I will confess my transgressions to the Lord," and You forgave the iniquity of my sin. For this cause everyone who is godly shall pray to You in a time when You may be found; surely in a flood of great waters they shall not come near him. You are my hiding place; You shall preserve me from trouble; You shall surround me with songs of deliverance* (Psalm 32:3-7).

There is one thing of which I am absolutely certain—God loves the prayer of repentance. He is waiting and ready to forgive before we even have time to finish our prayer. He wants, more than anything, that His children—you and me—would come to Him that they may be free to explore the wonders of their own gifts without the strength-sapping torment of sinner's guilt.

We can run to Him anytime. He forgives our sins and leads us into the right way of doing things.

He wants to answer our prayers no matter how insignificant we think they may be. He deals with the sin problems immediately so He can help us in our times of need.

From God's point of view, His arms are open to us and His love is always extended to His creation. He is always calling us to Himself. We should not hesitate to answer His call.

From our point of view, most of us know there are things that will keep us from praying effectively. We have trouble believing that God cares and will really answer our prayers. It is this sinner's torment that prevents us from having the assurance and confidence that He hears and will, most certainly, answer.

King David felt the same way when he was caught in sin with a soldier's wife and subsequently had the soldier killed to hide his sin.

Now there was a man in trouble. Yet King David understood enough about God to know he should run *to* Him and not *away from* Him. He knew God wanted to answer his prayers, so He simply repented to the God he loved and who loved him. Here is the king's prayer. Maybe you want to pray this prayer too.

Have mercy upon me, O God, according to Your lovingkindness; according to the multitude of Your tender mercies, blot out my transgressions. Wash me thoroughly from my iniquity, and cleanse me from my sin. For I acknowledge my transgressions, and my sin is always before me. Against You, You only, have I sinned, and done this evil in Your sight—that You may be found just when You speak, and blameless when You judge.

Behold, I was brought forth in iniquity, and in sin my mother conceived me. Behold, You desire truth in the inward parts, and in the hidden part You will make me to know wisdom. Purge me with hyssop, and I shall be clean; wash me and I shall be whiter than snow. Make me hear joy and gladness, that the bones You have broken may rejoice. Hide Your face from my sins, and blot out all my iniquities.

Create in me a clean heart, O God, and renew a steadfast spirit within me. Do not cast me away from Your presence, and do not take Your Holy Spirit from me. Restore to me the joy of Your generous Spirit. Then I will teach transgressors Your ways, and sinners shall be converted to You. Deliver me from the guilt of bloodshed, O God, the God of my salvation, and my tongue shall sing aloud of Your righteousness.

Oh Lord, open my lips, and my mouth shall show forth Your praise. For You do not desire sacrifice, or else I would give it; You do not delight in burnt offering. The sacrifices of God are a broken spirit, a broken and contrite heart—these, O God, You will not despise (Psalm 51:1-17.)

Praying that prayer from your heart to the Lord Jesus takes away the guilt of your sin. You can know with confidence that He loves you and wants to answer your prayers.

We can learn a lot from King David. Even though he had sinned so terribly, he could still experience God's love and power in his life. King David was not afraid to ask the Lord for anything, because he knew God loved him and wanted to answer his prayers.

The following are a few prayers—Psalms of David—that King David prayed after he asked God to forgive him. He was a man who understood that he really was free from the guilt of his sin. May we be assured of that promise from God as well.

> *Let God arise, let His enemies be scattered; let those also who hate Him flee before Him. As smoke is driven away, so drive them away; as wax melts before the fire, so let the wicked perish at the presence of God. But let the righteous be glad; let them rejoice before God; yes, let them rejoice exceedingly* (Psalm 68:1-3).

> *Give ear, O Lord, to my prayer; and attend to the voice of my supplications. In the day of*

my trouble I will call upon You, for You will answer me. Among the gods there is none like You, O Lord; nor are there any works like Your works. All nations whom You have made shall come and worship before You, O Lord; and shall glorify Your name. For You are great, and do wondrous things; You alone are God. Teach me Your way, O Lord; I will walk in Your truth; unite my heart to fear Your name (Psalm 86:6-11).

When our conscience is cleared and we are certain we are forgiven, our strength is renewed and our hearts are light. We have a sense of hope. We begin to dream again and the future is as bright as our present. But this not the end, for humanity is weak, unpredictable, and unfortunately, we are prone to fall back into our old way of life. But God even made a plan for that. It is what I call "broken repentance." It is the attitude that says, *"I know I am weak and know He forgives. I know He will give me strength to stand and the ability to resist temptation. But when I fail, I will not hesitate to run to Him in fresh repentance, in broken admission that I have failed the One I love and the One to whom I have committed my life."*

The lifestyle of broken repentance will always be your safety net, your hope, and your assurance that He always forgives, gathers, refreshes, answers, and will set you, once again, on the path He has chosen for you.

Section II

History's Darkest Hours Give Birth to Our Greatest Prayers

Don Milam Jr.

CHAPTER 5

History Proves the Power of Prayer

Humans have consistently rejected God and His involvement in their lives except when times have gotten really difficult. In our own strength and wisdom, we get ourselves into situations that require supernatural intervention to get out of, and at times some very dark situations.

But God is so gracious. He will always respond to the cries of His creation. But He responds for more than His love for us, although it is true that love always is the primary reason for Divine intervention. God has designed a destiny for each of us as individuals, therefore there is a special destiny on the nation where those individuals dwell.

God's plan, indeed, is to rescue us. But it is far deeper than that. He wants to rescue us so that our unique contribution for our planet can be made. Our destiny is wrapped up in our well-being. For when we are stable emotionally and spiritually we are free to devote our strength, creativity, and time to the things within that need to be sown over the earth, for His glory.

Humanity has consistently misunderstood God's love and consistently failed to understand that there is purpose and destiny within each person that must be poured out if the world is to not only be saved, but prosper, flourish, and live in peaceful harmony with all of God's creation.

The Birth of World-Changing Prayer

There is no doubt. The most effective prayers are born out of the most difficult of circumstances. The more difficult the plight, the more we direct our attention to that plight. The more we direct focus on the circumstances of the struggle, the clearer our need becomes and the more easily the prayer is formed in our hearts and flows out of our mouths with little thought of religious correctness or protocol.

That is how it should be. God is more interested in the authenticity of our prayers than He is the form. For the correct form is not the issue. The heart is and always will be the issue. He responds to a sincere and humble heart of prayer. Many have been incorrectly led to believe that the correct prayer, regardless of the condition of heart, will always bring an answer to our liking.

Of course, there are times of urgency when all we can do is blurt out the first thing that comes to mind. But I am speaking about something far deeper. I am speaking of prayer that is the result of calculated understanding, personal desire, and destiny. Our long-term success in prayer is always based on our long-term relationship with the One we are praying to. Yes, He will answer our prayers for help, deliverance, and health. But He also wants to answer our prayers for destiny, purpose, and personal spiritual growth.

Many are quick to run to God in times of deep physical and emotional peril. If their long-term relationship with God is not what it should be, our approach to Him is stifled. We are not sure what to say or how we can say it. We usually begin by making a long-term vow, we have no way to fulfill, when trying to gain His approval so He will answer us. It is far better, far safer, and far more rewarding to live a life of broken repentance. This lifestyle of humility and "teach-ableness" keeps the lines of communications open, powerful, and rewarding.

> *"It shall come to pass that before they call, I will answer; and while they are still speaking, I will hear. The wolf and the lamb shall feed together, and the lion shall eat straw like the ox; and dust shall be the serpent's food. They shall not hurt or destroy in all My holy mountain," says the Lord* (Isaiah 65: 24-25).

History has given birth to some very powerful prayers as prideful people were humbled by circumstances of their own doing. Some very effective prayers were the result of humble serv-anthood and some by deep personal pain. Some were the victims of awful atrocities and others were the perpetrators of atrocities. But in all these circumstances, what came forth were prayers that flowed from the heart of a repentant man or woman and moved the heart of God.

Prepare the Heart and Answers Follow

The prayers I am sharing with you are not intended to be the exact prayers you will want to pray. I present these person's prayers for several reasons. I want you to see their:

- softness of heart.
- honesty before God.
- very personal, individual ways of praying.
- boldness.
- faith in the incredible things they ask.
- unwavering confidence in God to answer.

It is certain that the preparation of the heart is the key to answered prayer. The purification of the motive, desire, and the soul will always give us assurance that we are praying as sincerely as we know how. By preparing our hearts on a daily basis, we will not only pray in faith but we will live by faith. This kind of lifestyle is devotional in nature and rewarding in peace, rest, and assurance in everyday living. For true peace comes in knowing we are not just talking aimlessly into the air, but that our loving heavenly Father, who instructs us what to pray, then gives us the faith to pray.

The following are some prayers others have prayed that helped them develop this pattern of peace in their lives.

Francis of Assisi (Catholic Monk, 1181-1226)
Lord, make me an instrument of your peace,
Where there is hatred, let me sow love;
Where there is injury, pardon;
Where there is doubt, faith;
Where there is despair, hope;
Where there is darkness, light;
Where there is sadness, joy;

O Divine Master, grant that I may not so much seek to be consoled as to console;
to be understood as to understand;
to be loved, as to love.
For it is in giving that we receive;
it is in pardoning that we are pardoned;
it is in dying that we are born to eternal life.

Keith Green (Christian singer/songwriter, 1953-1982)
Oh Lord, You're beautiful,
Your face is all I see,
For when Your eyes are on this child,
Your grace abounds to me.

Oh Lord, please light the fire,
That once burned bright and clean.
Replace the lamp of my first love,
That burns with holy fear.
I want to take Your Word and shine it all around.
But first help me just to live it, Lord.
And when I'm doing well, help me to never seek
a crown.
For my reward is giving glory to You.

Psalm 5:1-3, 7-8, 11-12

Give ear to my words, O Lord, consider my meditation. Give heed to the voice of my cry, my King and my God, for to You I will pray. My voice You shall hear in the morning, O Lord; in the morning I will direct it to You, and I will look up. But as for me, I will come into Your house in the multitude of Your mercy; in fear of You I will worship toward Your holy temple. Lead me, O Lord, in Your righteousness because of my enemies; make Your way straight before my face. But let all those rejoice who put their trust in You; let them ever shout for joy, because You defend them; let those also who love Your name be joyful in You. For You, O Lord, will bless the righteous; with favor You will surround him as with a shield.

The Columban Fathers (Columban.org)

May You always be my hope, my trust, my riches, my delight, my joy and gladness, my rest and quiet, my food, my refreshment, my refuge and help, my wisdom, portion and possession, my treasure in which my mind and heart shall be rooted forever, fixed, firm and immovable.

Psalm 63:1-8 (NASB)

O God, You are my God; I shall seek You earnestly; my soul thirsts for You, my flesh yearns for You, in a dry and weary land where there is no water. Thus I have seen You in the sanctuary, to see Your power and Your glory. Because Your lovingkindness is better than life, my lips will praise You. So I will bless You as long as I live; I will life up my hands in Your name. My soul is satisfied as with marrow and fatness, and my mouth offers praises with joyful lips. When I remember You on my bed, I meditate on You in the night watches, for You have been my help, and in the shadow of Your wings I sing for joy. My soul clings to You; Your right hand upholds me.

Psalm 26:4-5

Show me Your ways, O Lord; teach me Your paths. Lead me in Your truth and teach me, for You are the God of my salvation; on You I wait all the day.

Dr. Martin Luther King Jr., *"We Are Made for the High Places"*

God grant that under the spirit of Jesus Christ you will choose a high way. Eternal God our Father, we thank Thee for the inspiration of Jesus. Grant that we will follow His way and recognize that we are made for the high places. And grant that we will rise up out of the low, far countries of evil and return to the father's house. And now unto Him whom is able to keep us from falling and to present us faultless before our father's throne, to Him be power and authority, majesty and dominion, now, henceforth, and forevermore, Amen.[1]

Ignatius of Loyola

Dearest Lord, teach me to be generous;
Teach me to serve You as You deserve;
To give and not to count the cost,
To fight and not to heed the wounds,
To toil and not to seek for rest,
To labour and not to ask for reward,
Save that of knowing I am doing Your Will.[2]

Mother Teresa (Missionary of Compassion, 20th Century)

Dear Jesus, help us to spread your fragrance everywhere we go. Flood our souls with your spirit and life. Penetrate and possess our whole being so utterly that our lives may only be a radiance of yours. Shine through us and be so in us that every soul we come in contact with may feel your Presence in our soul. Let them look up and see no longer us, but only Jesus. Stay with us and then we shall begin to shine as you shine, so to shine as to be light to others. The light, O Jesus, will be all from you. None of it will be ours. It will be you shining on others through us. Let us thus praise you in the way you love best by shining on those around us. Let us preach you without preaching, not by words, but by our example; by the catching force—the sympathetic influence of what we do, the evident fullness of the love our hearts bear to you. Amen.[3]

Franklin D. Roosevelt (U.S. President, 20th Century) (Speech delivered June 6, 1944)
Almighty God: Our sons, pride of our nation, this day have set upon a mighty endeavor, a struggle to preserve our Republic, our religion, and our civilization, and to set free a suffering humanity. Lead them straight and true; give strength to their arms, stoutness to their hearts, steadfastness in their faith...fathers, mothers, children,

wives, sisters, and brothers of brave men over-
seas, whose thoughts and prayers are ever with
them—help us, Almighty God, to rededicate
ourselves in renewed faith in Thee in this hour
of great sacrifice. Many people have urged that I
call the nation into a single day of special prayer.
But because the road is long and the desire is
great, I ask that our people devote themselves in
a continuance of prayer. As we rise to each new
day, and again when each day is spent, let words
of prayer be on our lips, invoking Thy help to
our efforts.

Give us strength, too—strength in our daily
tasks, to redouble the contributions we make
in the physical and the material support of our
armed forces. And let our hearts be stout, to
wait out the long travail, to bear sorrows that
may come, to impart our courage unto our sons
wheresoever they may be. And, O Lord, give us
faith. Give us faith in Thee; faith in our sons;
faith in each other; faith in our united crusade.

Let not the keenness of our spirit ever be
dulled. Let not the impacts of temporary events,
of temporal matters of but fleeting moment—let
not these deter us in our unconquerable purpose.

With Thy blessing, we shall prevail over the unholy forces of our enemy. Help us to conquer the apostles of greed and racial arrogances. Lead us to the saving of our country, and with our sister nations into a world unity that will spell a sure peace—a peace invulnerable to the schemings of unworthy men. And a peace that will let all of men live in freedom, reaping the just rewards of their honest toil. Thy will be done, Almighty God. Amen.[4]

Thomas Merton (Catholic theologian, 20th Century)
When I am liberated by silence, when I am no longer involved in the measurement of life, but in the living of it, I can discover a form of prayer in which there is effectively no distraction. My whole life becomes a prayer. My whole silence is full of prayer. The world of silence in which I am immersed contributes to my prayer.[5]

Mary Queen of Scots (Queen of Scotland, 16th Century)
Lord my God, I hope in thee; My dear Lord Jesus, set me free; In chains, in pains, I long for thee; On bended knee I adore thee, implore thee To set me free.[6]

Thomas Jefferson (U.S. President, 18th Century)
God who gave us life gave us liberty. And can the liberties of a nation be thought secure when we have removed their only firm basis, a conviction in the minds of the people that these liberties are a gift from God?[7]

Queen Elizabeth I (Queen of England, 16th Century)
Lorde God Father everlasting, which reigneth over the Kingdoms of men…so teach me, I humbly beseech Thee, thy word, and so strengthen me with thy grace that I may feed thy people with a faithful and a true heart: and rule them prudently with power. Oh Lord, thou hast set me on high, my flesh is frail and weak. If I therefore at any time forget thee, touch my heart, o Lord, that I may again remember thee, if I swell against thee, pluck me down in my own conceit…. I acknowledge, oh my King, without thee my throne is unstable, my seat unsure, my Kingdom tottering, my life uncertain. I see all things in this life subject to mutability, nothing to continue still at one stay…. Create therefore in me, O Lord, a new heart, and so renew my spirit within me that thy law may be my study, thy truth my delight;

thy church my care; thy people my crown; thy
righteousness my pleasure; thy service my government...so shall this my kingdom through thee
be established with peace....[8]

Martin Luther King Jr. (Civil Rights Activist,
20th Century)
Well, I don't know what will happen now. We've
got some difficult days ahead. But it doesn't
matter with me now. Because I've been to the
mountaintop. And I don't mind. Like anybody,
I would like to live a long life. Longevity has its
place. But I'm not concerned about that now. I
just want to do God's will. And He's allowed me
to go up to the mountain. And I've looked over.
And I've seen the Promised Land. I may not get
there with you. But I want you to know tonight,
that we, as a people will get to the Promised
Land. And I'm happy, tonight. I'm not worried
about anything. I'm not fearing any man. Mine
eyes have seen the glory of the coming of the
Lord (April 3, 1968)[9]

Sir Walter Raleigh (Adventurer, Writer, 16th
century)
Give me my scallop-shell of quiet, my staff of faith
to walk upon, my scrip of joy, immortal diet, my

bottle of salvation, my gown of Glory, hope's true gage; and this I'll take my pilgrimage.[10]

Abraham Lincoln (U.S. President, 19th century)
I have been driven many times upon my knees by the overwhelming conviction that I had nowhere else to go. My own wisdom and that of all about me seemed insufficient for that day.[11]

Woodrow Wilson (U.S. President, 19th century)
I pray God I may be given the wisdom and the prudence to do my duty in the true spirit of this great people. I am their servant and can succeed only as they sustain and guide me by their confidence and their counsel. The thing I shall count upon, the thing without which neither counsel nor action will avail, is the unity of America—an America united in feeling, in purpose and in its vision of duty, of opportunity and of service.[12]

Francis of Assisi

You are holy, Lord, the only God, and Your deeds are wonderful. You are strong. You are great. You are the Most High. You are Almighty. You, Holy Father are King of heaven and earth. You are Three and One, Lord God, all Good. You are Good, all Good, supreme Good, Lord God, living and true. You are love. You are wisdom.

You are humility. You are endurance. You are rest. You are peace. You are joy and gladness. You are justice and moderation. You are all our riches, and You suffice for us. You are beauty. You are gentleness. You are our protector. You are our guardian and defender. You are our courage. You are our haven and our hope. You are our faith, our great consolation. You are our eternal life, Great and Wonderful Lord, God Almighty, Merciful Saviour.[13]

Michelangelo (Italian Artist, 16th Century)
Lord, make me see thy glory in every place: If mortal beauty sets my heart aglow, Shall not that earthly fire by thine burn low, Extinguisht by the great light of thy grace? Dear Lord, I cry for thee for help, O raise Me from the misery of this blind woe, Thy spirit alone can save me: let it flow Through will and sense, redeeming what is base.[14]

Beethoven (German Composer, 19th Century)
God give me strength to be victorious over myself, for nothing may chain me to this life. O guide my spirit, O raise me from these dark depths, that my soul, transported through Thy wisdom, may fearlessly struggle upward in fiery

flight. For Thou alone understandest and canst inspire.[15]

King Robert of France (11th Century)

O thou almighty Will, Faint are thy children, till Thou come with power; Strength of our good intents, In our frail home, Defence, Calm of Faith's confidence, Come, in this blessed hour! O thou most tender Love! Deep in our spirits move; Tarry, dear Guest! Quench thou our passion's fire, Raise thou each low desire, Deeds of brave love inspire, Quick-ener and Rest!

O Light serene and still! Come and our spirit fill, Bring in the day: Guide of our feeble sight Star of our darkest night, Shine on the path of right, Show us the way![16]

Thoughts, Advice, and Encouragement on Prayer[17]

Billy Graham (Evangelist, 20th century)

Prayer is the rope that pulls God and man together. But, it doesn't pull God down to us: It pulls us up to Him.

Corrie Ten Boom (Christian Activitist, Author)

Don't pray when you feel like it. Have an appointment with the Lord and keep it.

Abraham Joshua Heschel (American Jewish
Theologian)
In prayer we shift the center of living from
self-consciousness to self-surrender.

Abraham Lincoln
I have been driven many times to my knees by
the overwhelming conviction that I had nowhere
else to go. My own wisdom, and that of all about
me, seemed insufficient for the day.

Ronald Reagan (U.S. President, 20th century)
Prayer has sustained our people in crisis,
strengthened us in times of challenge, and guided
us through our daily lives since the first settlers
came to this continent. Our forbearers came not
for gold, but mainly in search of God and the
freedom to worship in their own way.[18]

Mahatma Gandhi (Leader of Indian
Independence Movement)
Prayer is not an old woman's idle amusement.
Properly understood and applied, it is the most
potent instrument of action.[19]

C. S. Lewis (Christian Writer)

He Himself is the fuel our spirits were designed to burn, or the food our spirits were designed to feed on. There is no other.[20]

Daniel Webster (U.S. Senator and Educator, 19th Century)

If we and our posterity reject religious instruction and authority, violate the rules of eternal justice, trifle with the injunctions of morality, and recklessly destroy the political constitution which holds us together, no man can tell how sudden a catastrophe may overwhelm us that shall bury all our glory in profound obscurity.[21]

Endnotes

1. Martin Luther King Jr.; Lewis V. Baldwin, ed., *"Thou, Dear God": Prayers that Open Hearts and Spirits* (Boston: Beacon Press, 2012).

2. Catholic Online; www.catholic.org/prayers/prayer.php?p=592; accessed September 26, 2015.

3. www.worldprayers.org.

4. www.historyplace.com/speeches/fdr-prayer.html; accessed September 26, 2015.

5. www.worldprayers.org.

6. Elizabeth Goudge, *A Diary of Prayer* (New York: Coward-McCann, 1966), 231.

7. www.prayforleaders.org/quotes.html

8. Barbara Greene and Victor Gollancz, *God of a Hundred Names* (Garden City, NY: Doubleday and Company, Inc., 1962), 105.

9. www.worldprayers.org.

10. Greene and Gollancz, 62.

11. Michael Burlingame, ed., *Lincoln Observed: The Civil War Dispatches of Noah Brooks*

(Baltimore, MD: Johns Hopkins University Press, 1998), 210.

12. Portion of Woodrow Wilson's 2nd Inaugural Address (1917).

13. Greene and Gollancz, 202.

14. www.worldprayers.org.

15. Greene and Gollancz, 207.

16. Goudge, 225.

17. www.worldprayers.org.

17. www.positiveprayers.org.

18. www.beliefnet.com.

19. www.beliefnet.com.

20. www.beliefnet.com.

21. Daniel Webster, *The Writings and Speeches of Daniel Webster* (Boston: Little, Brown, & Company, 1903, Vol. XIII, 492. From "The Dignity and Importance of History," February 23, 1852).

Psalm 116:1-9

I love the Lord, because He has heard my voice and my supplications. Because He has inclined His ear to me, therefore I will call upon Him as long as I live. The pains of death surrounded me, and the pangs of Sheol laid hold of me; I found trouble and sorrow. Then I called upon the name of the Lord; "O Lord, I implore You, deliver my soul!"

Gracious is the Lord, and righteous; yes, our God is merciful. The Lord preserves the simple; I was brought low, and He saved me. Return to your rest, O my soul, for the Lord has dealt bountifully with you.

For You have delivered my soul from death, my eyes from tears, and my feet from falling. I will walk before the Lord in the land of the living.

Section III

Patterns of Prayer

by Cleddie Keith

Psalm 121

I will lift up my eyes to the hills—
From whence comes my help?
My help comes from the Lord,
Who made heaven and earth.

He will not allow your foot to be moved;
He who keeps you will not slumber.
Behold, He who keeps Israel
Shall neither slumber nor sleep.

The Lord is your keeper;
The Lord is your shade at your right hand.
The sun shall not strike you by day,
Nor the moon by night.

The Lord shall preserve you from all evil;
He shall preserve your soul.
The Lord shall preserve your going out and
your coming in
From this time forth, and even forevermore.

CHAPTER 6

Why Prayer by Pattern?

Over the years I have found that patterns of prayer are very beneficial in helping me pray. Scripture makes it clear that from time to time we need to give instruction, or be instructed as to the matter of praying. Patterns help us organize our thoughts. They also help us focus on the Lord.

As a pastor, I have learned how to pray by praying. Talking to God with some guidance always helped me as I learned to commune with the Lord. The following pages are two recommended patterns of prayer which will be helpful to you on your prayer journey: The Ten Commandments and The Lord's Prayer.

Praying the Ten Commandments (Exodus 20:3-17)

We use this portion of Scripture as a pattern of prayer because we know that these instructions came straight from the heart of God to maintain order among humankind.

As in any pattern of prayer, you will think of other things to pray for as you use the following notes. Remember that a pattern will always help you in this way. As you pray according to a pattern, the Lord will bring many things to memory that you should remember in prayer. You may even find that you will not be able to pray through an entire pattern at one sitting. That is fine. The goal is to develop a spontaneous and vibrant conversation with the Lord. A pattern only helps you to get started.

First Commandment

You shall have no other gods before Me.
Today we honor You as the only God; there is none beside You. We honor You as our Creator. We honor You as sovereign Lord. We worship You as the only God, full of mercy and truth. There is none higher, none more wonderful than You. We praise Your wonderful name.

Second Commandment

You shall not make for yourself a carved image...you shall not bow down to them nor serve them. For I, the Lord your God, am a jealous God, visiting the iniquity of the fathers upon the children to the third and fourth generations of those who hate Me.

Anything that stands between you and God is an idol. We pray blessings and not curses upon our children, blessings to the fourth generation. We also pray blessings on our nation, our leaders, and our communities. We trust God for the best possible He has for them. Lord, help us to notice when something seems to be more important than You; when something comes between us and Your love and plan for us.

Third Commandment

You shall not take the name of the Lord your God in vain, for the Lord will not hold him guiltless who takes His name in vain.

God, You reveal Yourself to me through Your name. The Bible gives You several names. They all help me to understand who You really are and how much You really love me.

You are the Lord:

Jehovah-Tsidkenu—God is our Righteousness
(Jeremiah 23:5)

Jehovah-M'Kaddesh—*God* Sanctifies me
(Psalm 23:5)

Jehovah-Shalom—*God* is my Peace
(Psalm 23:2)

Jehovah-Shammah—God is Present
(Ezekiel 48:35)

Jehovah-Rophe—God is my Healer
(Psalm 30:2)

Jehovah-Jireh—God is my Provider
(Genesis 22:14)

Jehovah-Nissi—God is my Standard-Bearer
(Exodus 17:15)

Jehovah-Rohi—God is my Shepherd
(Psalm 23:1)

Fourth Commandment

Remember the Sabbath day, to keep it holy.
God Himself is my Sabbath or rest; and there remains a rest for the people of God (see Hebrews 4:9-10). I trust You, God, to do what I cannot

do. I want You, Lord. I rest in Your love, in Your provision. I refuse to be fearful. I refuse to panic. I rest in Your love for me.

Fifth Commandment

Honor your father and your mother, that your days may be long upon the land which the Lord your God is giving you.

We pray concerning the rebellion in the hearts of youth. Lord, I pray for the children, all children. Lord, please turn the hearts of the children back to their parents, back toward their families. Please mend the brokenness among families and help our children to have a heartfelt love and respect for their parents. (See Malachi 4:6.) We pray for parents, that their hearts would turn to their children; to love them, to raise them with honor and in the fear of the Lord.

Sixth Commandment

You shall not murder.

We pray for a respect for life across the United States of America. We take it as a personal assault on our faith when someone is murdered. We pray for domestic tranquility and harmony in every home. Lord, no one hates murder more than

You do. I pray for Your Presence in our cities and towns. But I also pray for Your Presence in our hearts so that the spirits of murder and death will have no place to rest. Let healing come to our hearts and to our land.

Seventh Commandment

You shall not commit adultery.

Oh Lord, I take authority over the spirit of lust that drives men and women to compromise their lives. We pray that the marriage beds will be undefiled and that men and women will look upon one another as temples of the Holy Spirit. I pray for holiness to be born in the hearts of all Your people. I pray that Your love will overcome the lust that so many fight and hate. May we see our spouses as the wonderful gifts from the Lord that they really are. Teach us to love them with everything that is in us.

Eighth Commandment

You shall not steal.

I pray that people will not steal but work with their hands. We pray that people will give an honest day's work for an honest day's pay. Lord, help me not to be greedy and envious of others.

You take wonderful care of me. Besides, if I need anything, all I have to do is ask You. You are my Provider. I love You. Thank You, Lord.

Ninth Commandment

You shall not bear false witness against your neighbor.

I pray that people will not become false witnesses against their neighbors. I pray that our reputations will be safe in the hands of others and vice versa. Help us to be truthful to ourselves and to You, Lord. You can only forgive us if we are honest with ourselves and with You. May truth grow up from the deepest part of our hearts. May I learn to love the truth and cherish it.

Tenth Commandment

You shall not covet your neighbor's house...nor anything that is your neighbor's.

I pray that people will find themselves content no matter what their situation. Help me to be content. Help me to rejoice with another's promotion or new car or whatever You bless them with. You give me everything I need. I am happy for Your provision. Thank You, Lord. I love You!

Praying the Lord's Prayer (Matthew 6:9-13)

When Jesus' disciples asked Him how to pray, He gave them a pattern of prayer, commonly referred to as the Lord's Prayer.

I remember my father buying a sewing machine for my mother. He thought he had really done something wonderful. He had—he had bought himself a new toy! My mom never used it, but my father became a pretty good tailor. He could make dresses and shirts or whatever he wanted to make. For the most part it was just a piece of furniture that brought us a lot of laughs over the years. He would buy a pattern for a dress and then he would improvise. My father was very creative. He built a beautiful horse trailer in the front driveway of our home. The pattern was in his head. It amazed me. The same is true for prayer. When you have a pattern, you make beautiful things happen.

As you pray the Lord's Prayer, remember it is our Father you are talking to. He is not off making worlds somewhere. He is not too busy for you. He is closer to you than your next breath. Praise Him for all His wonderful works. Prayer is like dancing. C. S. Lewis said, "As long as you are watching your feet you are not dancing—you are only learning to dance."

For several years I have prayed the Lord's Prayer in a systematic fashion. I have found this to be a pattern of prayer that my very creative heavenly Father can form into wonderful, surprising, and beautiful responses.

In this manner, therefore, pray: Our Father,

I praise You, God, that you are my loving Father. You are more than my Creator—You are Dad. You are the One and only Protector of my soul. I love You, Father. I worship You.

in heaven,

Isaiah 55:9 says the heavens are above the earth, and so are God's ways higher than ours. Lord, I seek guidance from Heaven's perspective. Jesus set the example by doing only what He saw His Father doing. I, too, know not what to do without Your loving Presence leading me. I cannot do this myself. I need the help that only comes from Heaven.

Hallowed be Your name.

You have revealed Yourself to us through Your name. I call upon You by the names through which You have revealed Yourself to humankind, Your children. Lord, You are everything I need and want. By Your name, all the demons on earth and in hell tremble. By Your name, nature comes under Your Lordship and people are healed. But most wonderfully, by Your name, average people like me can come to know You as Savior and Lord. Thank You, Lord, in Jesus' name, for forgiving me and loving me.

Your Kingdom come. Your will be done....

This is not a passive prayer! To pray this prayer means to stomp my foot and mean business. Every person has a will to surrender—for God to have His will, I have to surrender my will. To yield my will is to humble myself. I can be humiliated by others, but only I can humble myself (see James 4:10).

Give us this day our daily bread...

Jesus, You said Your source of food was to do the will of Your Father (see John 4:34). What satisfies me is to know that I satisfy Your purpose. You are my necessary Bread (see John 6:35). You are the Bread of Heaven, and You also want me to look to You for my daily natural provision.

Forgive us our debts, as we forgive our debtors....

It is necessary to forgive if I expect to be heard when I pray, so Lord, I choose to forgive. (See Matthew 18:21-35.)

Do not lead us into temptation, but deliver us from the evil one.

Jesus, You were driven into the wilderness of temptation. It was there that the enemy attempted to cause You to forget who You are, saying, *"If You are the Son of God..."* (Luke 4:3). If the enemy can get *me* to forget who I am, he can get me to do whatever he wants me to do. Who am I? I will declare who I am in Christ. (See Galatians 3:26; Romans 8:37; Revelation 1:6.)

Ephesians 4:27 says not to *"give place"* to the devil. This means do not give the enemy a legal right to be in your life. Areas where the enemy can enter are fear, hate, witchcraft, and sexual immorality.

For Yours is the Kingdom and the power and the glory....

Psalm 108:5 says that Your glory is over all the earth. The glory of God is over my family, my friends, my loved ones, those with whom I worship. I pray that You will spread Your wings over them and protect them.

Four Levels of Prayer

In addition to a variety of scriptural patterns of prayer, there are also a variety of levels of prayer. Here are four such levels: crisis praying, petitional praying, relational praying, and intercession.

Crisis Praying

Crisis praying is one of the most emotional levels of prayer. We realize that things are out of control and demand a miracle. At this point we do not stop to think that this is the prerequisite for miracles: things must be out of control. Jesus spoke to this issue in the story of Peter walking with Him on the water. (See Matthew 14:26-32.) Peter had taken his eyes off Jesus. When he saw his predicament and was beginning to sink, Peter cried out to the Lord, "Help me!"

That is a prayer that most of us have prayed at one time or another. Jesus, ever the Teacher, used the circumstance to teach Peter a valuable lesson. He reached out and saved Peter from the powerful waves, saying, "Why did you doubt?" The word *doubt* means to be pulled in two different directions. In times of crisis we may feel like we are being pulled apart.

It is a crisis when your automobile is hydro-planing down the highway at 60 miles an hour. That is not the time for a long pretentious prayer. The law of aerodynamics has taken over, and things are out of your control. "Jesus! Help!" is usually the order of the moment.

This is what is meant by crisis praying.

Petitional Praying

Petitional praying may be considered "to make a formal request," because the term is used in law and government concerning legal issues. The story of Esther is a story of petition. She knew the protocol of human government full well, and was valiant in her petition of the king. When she went into the presence of the king uninvited, she knew that her life was at risk; but she had a con-fidence that she had been born into the kingdom for such a moment. She made her petition at all costs by stating, *"If I perish, I perish"* (Esther 4:16). People who know their destiny are not afraid of taking risks. To petition in this case is to ask or to request.

First John 5:14-15 is an example of petitional prayer. It reads, *"Now this is the confidence that we have in Him, that if we ask anything according to His will, He hears us. And if we know that He hears us, whatever we ask, we know that we have the petitions that we have asked of Him."*

Relational Praying

Relational prayers are just what they imply. There is a relationship that exists between persons. Good relationships equal good communications. When my father died at an early age, my sister Karissa was only seven years old; his death shattered her world. My mother loved the Word of God. She knew it well and she knew Him well. I remember how she comforted my sister in those difficult days. I can still hear her say, *"Fear not, little flock; for it is your Father's good pleasure to give you the kingdom"* (Luke 12:32 KJV). My mother was laying down the true foundation for prayer in my sister's life.

Relational praying is talking to God as someone you have a relationship with, someone who loves you and has your best interest at heart. It is our privilege to come to Him as "Our Father." It is in this relationship that we can claim His

DON NORI SR.

promises, pardon, forgiveness, and grace, we can claim our daily bread; and we can claim a stingless death, and ultimately resurrection and an everlasting life.

Intercessory Prayer

To distinguish intercessory prayer from other types of prayer, it is necessary to define what is meant by the term intercessor. Intercessors are people who stand between—they are mediators. A more familiar term would be a lawyer.

Several years ago, I had to call on an attorney to take care of a legal situation for me. One day several weeks later, he called to say the matter was finished. I told him that I had learned something very valuable from him. He was curious as to how God had used him to teach me something. I told him that Jesus is revealed in the Scripture as the Advocate, and for a man to become a Christian, he must totally turn his case over to Him. There was silence on the phone that day and then I asked, "Friend, have you turned your case over to Him?"

Jesus is our chief example of what an intercessor really should be. He lives to make intercession for us. The Holy Spirit is ever-pleading our case to Jesus, and Jesus is ever-pleading our case to the Father. (See Hebrews 7:25; Romans 8:27.)

My father-in-law, Hardie Weathers, was a notorious intercessor and he taught me the importance of prayer. He reminded me of what David said in Psalm 109:4, *"I give myself to prayer."* Hardie would go to prayer just like a man would go to work on a secular job. He would break for lunch and then go back to the important ministry of prayer. I can still hear him say, "We learn to walk by walking, we learn to run by running, we learn to talk by talking, we learn to sing by singing, we learn to give by giving, and we learn to pray by praying."

Discovering the Power of Prayer

God wants to answer our prayers. He has proven that to me time and time again over the years. There is nothing He will not do for those who call to Him in sincerity and humility. I have seen broken marriages healed. I have watched as children angrily and tragically left their homes, only to return later in repentance and fresh love for their parents. I have seen people healed from the most terrible diseases, and I have seen hope restored to alcoholics and drug addicts. I have seen all this through the power of prayer—prayer that the Lord taught me as I prayed.

He will do the same for you. Take time to pray. Your heavenly Father loves you! He is waiting for you right now. Find a quiet place, close your eyes, think of your Father in Heaven and begin talking to Him as you would talk to your best friend. After all, you may not realize it yet, but He is your Best Friend.

Section IV

Lord, How Should We Pray? Prayers to Help You Talk to God

Dian Layton

The Lord's Prayer
Matthew 6:9-12 KJV

After this manner therefore pray ye:
Our Father which art in heaven,
Hallowed be thy name.
Thy kingdom come,
Thy will be done in earth,
As it is in heaven.
Give us this day our daily bread.
And forgive us our debts,
As we forgive our debtors.

CHAPTER 7

God Wants Us to Pray

God is waiting to hear you pray. Prayer is simply talking to God. The best prayers are the ones we say using our own words. The best prayers also are prayers that are not one-sided conversations. God wants to speak to you.

Learning to hear God's voice is an exciting adventure. His voice will come to you in many ways. He may come to you more as a feeling inside, like a nudging or an impression. You might see a picture in your mind, or you may suddenly have an idea that you know you didn't think up yourself.

In this section, we have provided a variety of prayers that are powerful and effective. This is just a starting place. As soon as you pray these prayers, many wonderful ideas and important things to pray for will come to your mind.

So, find a quiet place, get a pen and notebook, and be ready for a conversation with the Living God.

Prayer for Government Leaders

When the righteous are in authority, the people rejoice... (Proverbs 29:2).

Lord, You have the ultimate authority; You *are* the ultimate authority. You are high above all principality, and power, and might, and dominion, and every name that is named not only in this world, but also in that which is to come.

I pray for the leaders of our country. They need Your help, Lord! You've said in Your Word that if anyone lacks wisdom, all they need to do is ask; and You said there is safety in a multitude of counselors. So, I pray that every person in any position of authority will be led by Your Spirit. Give them wise counsel and wise counselors. Give them divine guidance. Help them to understand the times we are living in and show them the right course to take.

DON NORI SR.

Put a hedge of protection around every leader
and their family. Bless them, Lord! Bless them
with peace, prosperity, and an inner confidence
that You are in control. Amen.

> *Therefore I exhort first of all that suppli-*
> *cations, prayers, intercessions, and giving*
> *of thanks, be made for all men, for kings*
> *and for all who are in authority, that we*
> *may lead a quiet and peaceable life in all*
> *godliness and reverence* (1 Timothy 2:1-2).

See also 1 Chronicles 12:32, Isaiah 58:2,
Ephesians 1:21, James 1:5; 3:17, Proverbs 11:14.

Prayer for the Military

> *I will call upon the Lord, who is worthy*
> *to be praised; so shall I be saved from my*
> *enemies* (2 Samuel 22:4).

> *…nor do we know what to do, but our eyes*
> *are upon You* (2 Chronicles 20:12).

Save us from our enemies, Lord! Turn back the
forces that attack us, and rescue us from every
evil intention. Lord, we pray for all military per-
sonnel. Thank you for the men and women who

have stepped forward and reported for duty. Give them confidence, not in their own abilities, but in the fact that You are with them. Help them to realize how righteous the cause for battle really is. Give them courage and strength. In times when they are not sure what to do, may they turn their eyes and look to You for help. And may their families take comfort in Your Word:

> *Fear not, for I am with you; be not dismayed, for I am your God. I will strengthen you, yes, I will help you, I will uphold you with My righteous right hand. Behold, all those who were incensed against you shall be ashamed and disgraced; they shall be as nothing, and those who strive with you shall perish. You shall seek them and not find them—those who contended with you. Those who war against you shall be as nothing, as a nonexistent thing. For I, the Lord your God, will hold your right hand, saying to you, "Fear not, I will help you"* (Isaiah 41:10-13).

Prayer for Schools

> *The Spirit of the Lord shall rest upon Him,*
> *the Spirit of wisdom and understanding,*
> *the Spirit of counsel and might, the Spirit*
> *of knowledge and of the fear of the Lord.*
> *His delight is in the fear of the Lord, and*
> *He shall not judge by the sight of His*
> *eyes, nor decide by the hearing of His ears*
> (Isaiah 11:2-3).

Father God, I pray for our schools. Pour out Your Spirit and fill the children and young people of this nation with light that penetrates their darkness. I pray for Your protection and safety for each child, teacher, and administrator. Help us to keep praying for Your divine protection not only during these difficult days but also after these times pass by.

I pray for every Christian student and every Christian teacher. Give them strength to proclaim the truth in the midst of a so-called secular society that is filled with people longing to know You. Help them realize they are ambassadors for the King of kings. Give them a sense of destiny and purpose. As citizens of Heaven, they are representing You here on earth. Give them divine protection and holy boldness to declare You in every classroom, every office, every hallway, and every playground across the nations.

You told us to pray, "Let Your kingdom come," and that is what we pray for the schools around the world and in this country too. Let Your kingdom come and let Your will be done! Be high and lifted up across this land and draw thousands and thousands of young people to You. Amen!

Now then, we are ambassadors for Christ, as though God were pleading through us: we implore you on Christ's behalf, be reconciled to God (2 Corinthians 5:20).

And I, if I am lifted up from the earth, will draw all peoples to Myself (John 12:32).

Whom will he teach knowledge? And whom will he make to understand the message? Those just weaned from milk? Those just drawn from the breasts? For precept must be upon precept, precept upon precept, line upon line, line upon line, here a little, there a little (Isaiah 28:9-10).

All your children shall be taught by the Lord; and great shall be the peace of your children (Isaiah 54:13).

The eyes of your understanding being enlightened; that you may know what is the hope of His calling, what the riches of the glory of His inheritance in the saints, and what is the exceeding greatness of His power toward who believe, according to the working of His mighty power (Ephesians 1:18-19).

Prayer for the Children

All your children shall be taught by the Lord, and great shall be the peace of your children (Isaiah 54:13).

Jesus, You never change. You are the same yesterday, today, and forever. When You walked on this earth, You took young children in Your arms, put Your hands upon them, and blessed them.

Now we're asking You to touch our children. Take them in Your arms, put Your hands on them, and bless them, Lord! Fill their hearts with peace, and fill them with Your Holy Spirit. Fill them with joy and love, and with the confidence and power to do what is right.

Bless them, protect them, and keep Your hand upon their lives. Lord, we cannot be with them every minute of the day, but You can be with them and You are with them. Send Your angels to watch our children and to keep them safe.

And Lord, not only do we ask for Your protection, we also ask You to use our children. Your Word says that from the mouths of children comes praise so powerful that it silences the enemy. Well, the voice of the enemy has been much too loud in this generation! May the voices of children across this nation be lifted up with praise so powerful that it silences the enemy! May this generation of children be a generation who know You, Lord. Amen.

Jesus Christ is the same yesterday, today, and forever (Hebrews 13:8).

Jesus said, "Let the little children come to Me, and do not forbid them; for of such is the kingdom of heaven." And He laid His hands on them... (Matthew 19:14-15).

Take heed that you do not despise one of these little ones, for I say to you that in heaven their angels always see the face of My Father who is in heaven (Matthew 18:10).

Out of the mouth of babes and [young children] *You have ordained strength, because of Your enemies, that You may silence the enemy and the avenger* (Psalm 8:2).

And it shall come to pass afterward that I will pour out My Spirit on all flesh; your sons and your daughters shall prophesy, your old men shall dream dreams, your young men shall see visions. (Joel 2:28; see also Acts 2:17).

Arise, cry out in the night...pour out your heart like water before the face of the Lord. Lift your hands toward Him for the life of your young children... (Lamentations 2:19).

Prayer for Families

He will feed His flock like a shepherd; He will gather the lambs with His arm, and carry

*them in His bosom, and shall gently lead
those who are with young* (Isaiah 40:11).

The families of our nation need You, Lord! In a world of brokenness and division, we pray according to the last verse of the Old Testament: *"Turn the hearts of the fathers to the children, and the hearts of the children to their fathers"* (Malachi 4:6).

God, we ask You to turn the hearts of parents and children toward each other and toward You. In a world of confusion and uncertainty, our homes can be places of security and rest if You are there, Lord Jesus. When You are the central Person in our homes, You will give us inner confidence, no matter what is going on outside.

We pray that fathers and mothers will be the pastors of their homes. As they shepherd their little flock—Jesus, be their Shepherd, also. Gently lead parents. Give them wisdom in raising their children. Give them patience. And give them an extraordinary ability to see beyond the daily routines of life into the future.

Help parents realize that the days of childhood are precious days of planting seeds. The lives of their children are tender fields. Help parents to plant carefully and with purpose so that their children will have all they need to become all that You have intended for them.

You do have intentions for our children and for our families. You have dreams and plans for our futures that are very, very good. You are knocking on the door of each home, and on every heart. Help us to say, "Come in, Lord Jesus! Come in and be King and Shepherd and Savior of our lives. Amen."

Behold, I stand at the door and knock. If anyone hears My voice and opens the door, I will come in to him and dine with him, and he with Me (Revelation 3:20).

And He will turn the hearts of the fathers to the children, and the hearts of the children to their fathers, lest I come and strike the earth with a curse (Malachi 4:6).

And I will give you shepherds [pastors] *according to My heart, who will feed you with knowledge and understanding* (Pastor your family) (Jeremiah 3:15).

For I know the thoughts that I think toward you, saith the Lord, thoughts of peace and not of evil, to give you a future and a hope (Jeremiah 29:11).

You shall teach them to your children, speaking of them when you sit in your house, when you walk by the way, when you lie down, and when you rise up. And you shall write them on the doorposts of your house and on your gates, that your days and the days of your children may be multiplied in the land of which the Lord swore to your fathers to give them, like the days of the heavens above the earth (Deuteronomy 11:19-21).

Prayer for Comfort

He heals the brokenhearted, and binds up their wounds (Psalm 147:3).

Jesus, You said, "Blessed are they who mourn: for they shall be comforted." I'm claiming that promise today, Lord, because I really, really need to be comforted.

You said that Your Holy Spirit is "the Comforter." Well, here I am, Holy Spirit, asking You to comfort me. Wrap me up in the soft blanket of Your Presence. Cover me and hide me and heal my heart.

Your Word gives me comfort and hope. So, right now, I want to pray Psalm 23 in my own words, as if it were written just to me:

Lord, You are my Shepherd; I will not lack any good thing.

You let me rest in green pastures: You lead me beside clear, peaceful streams. You restore and renew the very essence of who I am.

You guide me in the right way and I pray that I will bring honor to Your name.

Even when I walk through the valley of the shadow of death, I will not be afraid because You are with me; Your guidance and protection comfort me. You set a banquet before me—right in the middle of trouble!

You anoint me and fill me to overflowing with Your Holy Spirit.

I am confident that goodness and mercy will be with me all the days of my life:

And I will live in Your Presence forever.

Amen.

For whatever things were written before were written for our learning, that we through patience and comfort of the Scriptures might have hope (Romans 15:4).

But the Helper, the Holy Spirit, whom the Father will send in My name, He will teach you all things, and bring to your remembrance all things that I said to you. Peace I leave with you, My peace I give to you; not as the world gives do I give to you. Let not your heart be troubled, neither let it be afraid (John 14:26-27).

Blessed are those who mourn, for they shall be comforted (Matthew 5:4).

Prayer for Courage

I would have lost heart, unless I had believed that I would see the goodness of the Lord in the land of the living. Wait on the Lord; be of good courage, and He shall strengthen your heart; wait, I say, on the Lord! (Psalm 27:13-14)

Give me courage, Lord. Give me the ability to keep going and to never give up. Help me realize that You really are God and that You really do control all things. I believe that I will yet see Your goodness in this land, in my family, and in my heart. You will complete what You have begun. You will not give up.

Give me courage, Lord. Give me the ability to see beyond my circumstances. Help me to lift my eyes higher and look at what I cannot see. By an act of my will, I choose to look at You. You made Heaven and earth. Your Word says that You call every star by name and that You hold everything in place by the Word of Your power. In all that greatness, You have also promised never to leave or forsake me.

With You on my side, what do I have to fear? With You on my side, who can be against me?! The choice before me is simple. I choose to trust in You with all my heart. I choose to be very courageous, knowing that God will give strength to my heart. Amen!

See also Psalm 121:1-2, Psalm 147:4, Philippians 1:6, 2 Corinthians 4:18, Colossians 1:16, Romans 8:31.

Prayer for Help

Let us therefore come boldly to the throne of grace, that we may obtain mercy and find grace to help in time of need (Hebrews 4:16).

God is our refuge and strength, a very present help in trouble (Psalm 46:1).

Lord, I need help. In the past, when I needed help, I ran to the refrigerator. Sometimes I ran to the shopping mall. Sometimes I ran to the television set, trying to hide my desperate need behind a world of fantasy; or I climbed back into bed, hoping sleep would provide an escape.

Not so today. Today I run to You. I run to You and cry out in my time of need. I pour out my trouble and my complaint. I ask You to somehow intervene in my circumstances before they completely overcome me. I need a miracle. Show me what to do! Provide a way for things to work out; make a way where there seems to be absolutely no way.

Help me, Lord! Amen.

Trust in Him at all times, you people; pour out your heart before Him; God is a refuge for us (Psalm 62:8).

For I, the Lord your God, will hold your right hand, saying to thee, "Fear not, I will help you" (Isaiah 41:13).

See also Psalm 102:1; 121:1-2; 124:7-8.

Prayer for Strength

And He said to me, "My grace is sufficient for you, for My strength is made perfect in weakness." Therefore most gladly I will rather boast in my infirmities, that the power of Christ may rest upon me. Therefore I take pleasure in infirmities, in reproaches, in needs, in persecutions, in distresses, for Christ's sake. For when I am weak, then I am strong (See 2 Corinthians 12:9-10.)

Lord, I'm so tired. I just can't do this anymore…

When I say those words, I can hear Your response, Lord: That's right. You can't. Now… will you let Me? I guess that's exactly what You meant when You said, *"My strength is made perfect in weakness."* I really won't experience Your strength until I reach the end of my own. Well, I've reached that end, Lord. I'm worn out and tired. My heart is so overwhelmed that I can't even find my way to You. So please lead me. Lead me into Your Presence, and wash away my weariness.

I stand here before You, and I lift my hands. I need You, Jesus. I cannot go another step until You strengthen me. Here, from the end of the earth, I cry out to You! Strengthen my heart! Strengthen my body! Strengthen my mind! Strengthen my love for You! Amen.

See also Psalm 31:24, 61:2; Isaiah 40:29,31.

Prayer for Wisdom

...that you may be filled with the knowledge of His will in all wisdom and spiritual understanding (Colossians 1:9).

If any of you lacks wisdom, let him ask of God, who gives to all liberally and without reproach, and it will be given to him (James 1:5).

Lord, You are Wisdom. You know absolutely everything. You know the beginning and the end. You know the thoughts of every person, and You know what the future will bring. You created us to live each day, walking and talking with You; but sadly, we most often choose to struggle through our lives without You.

I don't want to live like that. I want You to be intensely involved with my daily life. I want to hear Your voice saying, "This is the way, go here, or go there…do this, or do that…" Teach me to hear Your voice. Teach me to recognize the many ways You communicate with me; and help me to respond quickly to Your direction.

Life lived in constant communication with the Creator of the universe—that is how I will have wisdom. I want to begin today. Right now, I surrender control of every decision and every plan to You, Lord Jesus. I choose not to trust my own understanding, but to trust You. Amen.

See also Psalm 32:8, Proverbs 2:3-6, 3:5-7; Isaiah 30:21.

Prayer for Peace

The earth was without form, and void; and darkness was on the face of the deep. And the Spirit of God was hovering over the face of the waters. Then God said, "Let there be light"; and there was light (Genesis 1:2-3).

Lord, I know that at creation, the world was a chaotic mass. That is exactly the way my world seems sometimes: unorganized, empty, and really, really dark. Lord, I need You to speak to my world! I need You to say, "Let there be Light!" You spoke to Your disciples in the boat, when they were in a huge storm. Their world was certainly looking dark and chaotic...and there, in the middle of their distress, they called out to You. You stood up and spoke directly to the storm: "Peace. Be still." And the winds and the waves went calm.

So right now, I cry out to You in my distress. I pour out my trouble and my complaint and my fears—and right now, I hear You speaking those same words to me, "Peace. Be still." I see Your hand stretched toward my circumstances, and I see the winds and waves growing calm. Thank You for Your peace. Thank You for answering me in times of trouble. And thank You for always being with me. Amen.

And He arose and rebuked the wind, and said to the sea, "Peace, be still!" And the wind ceased and there was a great calm (Mark 4:39).

See also Psalm 18:6, 142:2; John 14:27; Philippians 4:7.

Getting to Know God

[God] *has in these last days spoken to us by His Son, whom He has appointed heir of all things, through whom also He made the worlds; who being the brightness of His glory and the express image of His person, and upholding all things by the word of His power, when He had by Himself purged our sins, sat down at the right hand of the Majesty on high* (Hebrews 1:2-3).

God really, really loves you. Yes, you! This book is about prayer. Praying is communication with God, and it's not one-sided conversation. God wants to reveal His love for us; He wants to speak to us. And when God talks, He doesn't just use words. He also uses pictures, visions, ideas, dreams, melodies, symbolic actions…

God spoke to us in the form of His Son, Jesus Christ. He was the greatest message the world has ever received. He is a message from the Creator of the universe, saying, "I love you." God loves you so much that He took upon Himself the form of a mere mortal man, and humbled Himself—not only to walk on this earth in human flesh, but also to die. Have you heard His message? Have you responded?

Here is a simple prayer to pray:

God, I want to know You. I have heard about You. I have prayed to You. But I have never really entered into the kind of relationship where You speak to me and I recognize Your voice. You revealed Yourself to this world as the Man Christ Jesus. I believe that. I believe that Jesus walked on this earth. I believe He died on the cross. And, I believe it was a personal message—to me. I want to say yes to Your invitation of friendship. I want to live each day in a relationship with You. And I have a feeling deep inside that my life is actually just beginning!

> *...I* [Jesus] *have come that they might have life, and that they might have it more abundantly* (John 10:10).

Being in the form of God...made Himself of no reputation, taking the form of a bondservant, and coming in the likeness of men. And being found in appearance as a man, He humbled Himself, and became obedient to the point of death, even the death of the cross (Philippians 2:7-8).

And this is life eternal, that they might know You, the only true God, and Jesus Christ whom You have sent (John 17:3).

After You Pray

During your prayer time, many other thoughts will come to mind. Those thoughts are prayer concerns of your heart. Take a few minutes to write them down and then begin to pray for them in your own words.

The more we talk to God, the more He wants to talk to us. After you have prayed, take a few minutes to listen quietly. You may be surprised by what you hear the Lord saying to you. His words always comfort and encourage us. They always draw us closer to Him.

Think of some people who need you to pray each prayer for them. List them by name.

Please use the journal pages we provided for you at the back of the book.

Section V

The Power of a
Praying Nation

Don Nori

Psalm 130

Out of the depths I have cried to You, O Lord;
Lord, hear my voice!
Let Your ears be attentive
To the voice of my supplications.

If You, Lord, should mark iniquities,
O Lord, who could stand?

But there is forgiveness with You,
That You may be feared.

I wait for the Lord, my soul waits,
And in His word I do hope.
My soul waits for the Lord
More than those who watch for the morning—
Yes, more than those who watch for the morning.

O Israel, hope in the Lord;
For with the Lord there is mercy,
And with Him is abundant redemption.
And He shall redeem Israel
From all his iniquities.

CHAPTER 8

Our God-Ordained Purpose

Why does a nation go to prayer? What can be the motivation behind such a noble endeavor?

Does a nation go to prayer simply to cry out for a respite from the ills that beset her? Is it enough for her to go to prayer only for deliverance from a foreign threat? Do we invoke the name of the Lord only when in peril, hastily going to Him in whatever method appears to bring the most immediate response? If this is our perception of His love and *if* we believe that this *is* the purpose for His existence, we are sadly missing the point altogether.

Is our purpose for being here so self-indulging? Is our vision so temporal? Is our future so mundane? I think not. No, we go to the Lord in prayer as a nation not seeking a temporary audience with the Almighty simply to plead our case for personal survival. We go to Him with the knowledge—no, with the conviction—that we are all here for a God-ordained purpose. We go to Him because we know that He can use us as individuals in this nation for the well-being of the entire community of nations. We are a motivated people. Because we are blessed by God with so much as well as the freedom to express our faith, to live it and give freely to others, we are compelled to bless the people of all nations.

You are here for a God-ordained purpose.

We are not here simply to procreate, as though our destiny is merely the survival of our species from one generation to the next. We are not wandering aimlessly throughout time, arbitrarily finding ourselves here in this country instead of somewhere else.

We are aware. We are attentive. We understand. We live. We laugh when we live and we mourn when we die. Each of us holds in our bosom, no matter how secretly, the under-standing, the confession, the hope that we are here for a purpose greater than mere random natural selection. Most understand that they are here by the finger of God. That we were purpose-fully made by the loving hands of our Father in Heaven. We have been placed where we are to be the most good, to do the most good, and to express the love of God that others may also do their most good.

The contribution that God has woven within us cannot be easily dismissed. For it is essential for the strength and well-being of all things living. One merely needs to look briefly at the condition of our planet to understand that most contributions of each individual has gone to the grave with them, thus robbing the world of its mighty benefit. A life cut short is rightfully mourned for a life not lived. But we would be far more attentive to life, to all life, if we understood the impact of losing the gift that each life is to the planet.

Far too many people, for far too many years have forgotten their birthright—both spiritual and physical. They have abdicated their calling and purpose for the temporal, experiencing momentary gratification over eternal value. Individual destiny has been replaced by individual personal and immediate gratification. The thrill of the moment has replaced the purpose, the calling, the destiny of a lifetime.

We sell our inheritance for a cup of soup with little realization of what we have sacrificed. Our young people cry out for purpose, but we give them games, rote entertainment to ease the monotonous passing of time in an aimless attempt to quell the destiny within them that yearns for expression. We have become so numb to the reality of our ever-present Lord that we struggle to know that there is something beyond flesh and blood.

How pertinent the words of Jesus are at this moment in time! How serious the pronouncement on a people who have not heeded the call of their Lord deep within! Jesus said, *"But to what shall I liken this generation? It is like children sitting in the marketplaces and calling to their companions, and saying: 'We played the flute for you, and you did not dance; we mourned to you, and you did not lament'"* (Matthew 11:16-17).

Wake-Up Call to the World

Unfortunately, it often takes tragedy to re-ignite the outward expression of the inner knowledge of who we really are beyond our humanity, beyond our flesh and blood. Misfortune is the breeding ground for revival of the heart and the troubles that follow us are our hope for daily fellowship with God. Humanity will always resort to our basic instincts, in general. The prudent turn to God in times of trouble and uncertainty. The greater the need for repentance, the greater the adversity.

Sometimes we respond to God and run to Him for shelter. But when a society does not acknowledge God and works to remove Him from the public discourse of everyday life, we will be left alone. We are limited to our own ability, our base instinct to survive, much like an animal has only base instincts. It is an amazing thought. An animal cannot turn to God for help and humankind often does not want to admit our need for a Higher Power in our lives.

Lesser species have no sense of destiny beyond their need to survive. They are unaware of anything more. In fact, our sense of destiny is the very thing that separates humanity from the rest of God's creation. For us, staying alive is much more than survival; it is much more than instinctively doing what comes naturally.

Humanity exists as part of a larger plan, carrying the absolute understanding that there exists above us a power transcending time and space. This power dwells in and passes through a dimension that is truly grasped only by faith and experienced by the humility of prayer and personal confession. But far more than merely a cosmic power way out there somewhere, God is a living, personal, vibrant Spirit who personally loves humanity and covets relationship with them.

So running to Him in panic only when He is needed will not do over the long term. Of course, He will always forgive us and take care of us when we ask Him. The Bible is full of examples of the Lord coming to the aid of His people when they were in great adversity. But there is more to this God than merely 911 calls. He made us because He loves us, because He wants our friendship, because He invested Himself in us for His purposes and plan for humankind. Our destiny is Divine in calling and complete in its fulfillment.

The need to fulfill our reason to breathe is the most driving passion in the universe.

Over the long term, being in fellowship with our God on a daily basis makes a whole lot more sense than running to Him, assuming you can find Him, when an emergency arises. This kind of "foul weather friendship" is not what we humans particularly enjoy from one another. Why do we think it is any different with God? He is devoted to a relationship with us based on mutual love and desire.

It is amazing how we think we can go on from one generation to the next, with less and less consideration for the One who made us for His pleasure. We cannot do this thing alone. We cannot survive as a nation (without considering our destiny) by calling to Him as a last resort to solve all our problems. He is much more exciting as One who unfolds His plan in us daily and strengthens us for the task. He is much more appealing as the One who loves and heals and blesses than as the One who must respond only in a crisis, only to have us forget Him again until the next problem arises.

The self-seeking, self-indulgence people of a nation concerned only with its immediate needs denies the greater purpose for our existence. Do we want to merely survive, or do we want to fulfill our reason for being born, in all its wonder and adventure? Life does not have to be boring, empty, devoid of purpose. We were not created to try to fill the emptiness within. Turning our hearts to our Lord in committed repentance and humility opens our heart for the life He intended for every human being to experience. This is what awaits you. This is the beginning of destiny...your destiny.

Let's Decide Together

Let's decide to pray in the times of crisis, as we all should do as a matter of course. But let us also make the decision to walk circumspectly, serving the God we expect to help us. For He is One with far more than just immediate help for us. He carries in His heart, destiny itself—for you, for your children, and for the nation. If we only understood what that means for each of us, our lives would be transformed forever.

There is no turning back to what was. The world is changing whether we like it or not. But we can be part of a growing force of Divine intervention that is the result of those who will pray.

Psalm 91

He who dwells in the secret place of the Most High
Shall abide under the shadow of the Almighty.
I will say of the Lord, "He is my refuge and my
fortress;
My God, in Him I will trust."

Surely He shall deliver you from the snare of the
fowler
And from the perilous pestilence.
He shall cover you with His feathers,
And under His wings you shall take refuge;
His truth shall be your shield and buckler.
You shall not be afraid of the terror by night,
Nor of the arrow that flies by day,
Nor of the pestilence that walks in darkness,
Nor of the destruction that lays waste at noonday.

A thousand may fall at your side,
And ten thousand at your right hand;
But it shall not come near you.
Only with your eyes shall you look,
And see the reward of the wicked.

Because you have made the Lord, who is my refuge,
Even the Most High, your dwelling place,
No evil shall befall you,
Nor shall any plague come near your dwelling;
For He shall give His angels charge over you,
To keep you in all your ways.
In their hands they shall bear you up,
Lest you dash your foot against a stone.
You shall tread upon the lion and the cobra,
The young lion and the serpent you shall trample
underfoot.

"Because he has set his love upon Me, therefore I
will deliver him;
I will set him on high, because he has known My
name.
He shall call upon Me, and I will answer him;
I will be with him in trouble;
I will deliver him and honor him.
With long life I will satisfy him,
And show him My salvation."

Do Not Ignore Your Contribution!

G od has dreamed a Divine dream for your life that will allow your individual contribution to the earth to be made and received. The dream He has for you is one only you can fulfill, for it was personally woven into your spiritual DNA when God made you. It is unique to your calling and much like a piece to a puzzle. There are lots of pieces, and the picture is not complete if each piece does not find its place where it belongs. You are just that unique.

And hear me carefully. Each of us has an important contribution to give. We were born with it. When we were formed in our mothers' womb by the hand of God, that contribution was written into our natural and spiritual DNA. It is woven into our very existence for He knew His plan for us when we were but a thought in His eternal heart.

Each person has value. No matter what troubles people have had, no matter their position in life, their education, their finances or their family, each person has an essential contribution to deposit while here on earth. Each person has something specific and something tangible to give for the benefit of all. It is simply true.

We, individually, are important to the advancement and success our world. We are essential to the well-being of the nations. To be sure, most are too myopic to see how one person in a small corner of the world with no money, no influence can possibly see their individual importance.

Yet, we are all connected in a spiritually wonderful way. Your success is my success. Your dreams fulfilled are every person's dreams fulfilled. When we succeed as individuals, we succeed as a species. When we succeed as a species it is because we succeed as individuals.

Your dreams fulfilled are every person's dreams fulfilled.

Your life cannot be measured by the limits of what your five senses show you. That standard of measure is grossly inadequate. Your affect on the world cannot be calculated by the number of friends you have. Your life cannot be marginalized by those who do not see the whole of God's plan for this planet. Your influence, your voice, your life, no matter how broadly it is seen or how narrow its apparent scope, has a profound effect on the world—your world.

You are assigned to the folks around you. Love them, care for them. Pray for them. Treat them the way you want to be treated. Love them with the love with which you want to be loved. Your impact on this tiny planet is magnified in ways you can never calculate when you give yourself to others in the ways of love.

Some may wonder why this is so important in a book on prayer. That is a good question. One must understand that prayer is motivated by the love, the attitudes, the desires of the heart. When the heart is full of the love, that is, the same kind of love that we want others to have for us, our prayer life will naturally change. No longer do we harbor thoughts and attitudes toward anyone that tear down rather than build up. Thoughts of envy, greed, and revenge melt away in the presence of His love in your heart. Forgiveness, hope, gratitude, and compassion become the very foundations that launch our prayers into the heart of God. For when love rules within, your prayers will most certainly reflect the love of God, which means your prayers will most certainly reflect the heart of God toward the issues for which you pray. I cannot think of another way to be confident that my prayers will be answered as when I am praying in the love and compassion of God Himself.

When your love releases prayer, your prayer, in turn, releases love. When love is released, so is your gift, your contribution to the planet. God sent you here as a gift that has far more value than you can realize. I spent many years dismissing who I was because no one else seemed to see what I saw. But then I had a startling epiphany. As long as I saw what I was and God saw what He had put within me, that was all that was needed. I believed in myself and God believed in me too. It was the beginning of a journey that has brought me to this place today. I am writing and you are reading what I am writing. My contribution is releasing your contribution and giving you courage and confidence to step out in ways you would have maybe never had imagined was possible.

You, too, are a source of inspiration and encouragement. Your contribution, no matter what it may be, is exactly what many, many folk need in their lives to also succeed. You have more value than you can possibly imagine. You have greater purpose and influence than you have thought. The world does not just need you, it is waiting for you. Your love, your smile, your hopeful words, your persistence, compassion, and love are invaluable contributions that will open your heart to do things for which the world desperately awaits.

Lift up your heart to your Lord.
Lift up your voice in prayer.
Lift up your hands in Divine surrender to Him.
The world will change before your eyes as you
release your contribution to it.
Boom.
You win.

What is mankind that You are mindful of them, human beings that You care for them? You have made them a little lower than the angels and crowned them with glory and honor. You made them rulers over the works of Your hands... (Psalm 8:4-6 New International Version).

Journal

Journal

_____

_____

_____

_____

_____

_____

_____

_____

_____

_____

_____

_____

_____

_____

_____

_____

Journal

_____

_____

_____

_____

_____

_____

_____

_____

_____

_____

_____

_____

_____

_____

Journal

_____

_____

_____

_____

_____

_____

_____

_____

_____

_____

_____

_____

_____

_____

_____

_____

Journal

_____

_____

_____

_____

_____

_____

_____

_____

_____

_____

_____

_____

_____

_____

_____

Journal

_____

_____

_____

_____

_____

_____

_____

_____

_____

_____

_____

_____

_____

_____

_____

Journal

_____

_____

_____

_____

_____

_____

_____

_____

_____

_____

_____

_____

_____

_____

_____

_____

Journal

_____

_____

_____

_____

_____

_____

_____

_____

_____

_____

_____

_____

_____

_____

_____

_____

Journal

_____

_____

_____

_____

_____

_____

_____

_____

_____

_____

_____

_____

_____

_____

_____

_____

Journal

_____

_____

_____

_____

_____

_____

_____

_____

_____

_____

_____

_____

_____

_____

About the Author

Don Nori Sr. is a driven man. The same passion for Jesus that arrested him more than forty years ago is the passion that led him to start Destiny Image Publishers in 1983 and is still the primary overshadowing power in his life today. Along with Cathy, his wife of more than forty-three years, they pursue life enthusiastically in the beautiful Cumberland Valley of central Pennsylvania. They spend much of their time happily spoiling their grandchildren and enjoying their sons and their wives. Don will probably write as long as God gives him breath.

THE
FORGOTTEN
MOUNTAIN

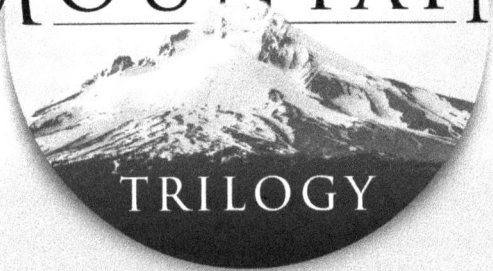

TRILOGY

The Forgotten Mountain

— BOOK ONE —

There is a reason believers struggle more than they should. There is a reason that there is so much pain, loss and heartache. It is not because we are destined to suffer because we are not. It is because we have forgotten the Mountain of the House of the Lord, the place of true inner governance under the rule of our King. He must increase and we must decrease. The Canaan life style is waiting as surely as it was waiting for ancient Israel to cross the river Jordan. We reign when we die...to ourselves.

After Pentecost

— BOOK TWO —

When ancient Israel fled the bondage of Egypt, they found solace in the wilderness. But it did not last long. They wandered in the waste places and wondered why it had to be so. But it didn't have to be so. They were called to pass through the wilderness as are called to pass through Pentecost into our Canaan in this life. Who will have the courage to leave the familiar, the secure, the visible evidence of His presence, opting for the authentic inner governance of the King; the establishing the permanent throne of His Kingdom within?

An Uncommon Revival

— BOOK THREE —

The lifestyle of the believer in Canaan is far different from the lifestyle of the wilderness that the ancient Israelites experienced. It is also far different from the life experienced in Pentecost. In this dimension of life, the King reigns, His presence tangible from within and the attributes of the King flow like water from the surrendered life. Here, destiny is fulfilled, the contribution of every man is appreciated and authentic Divine harmony begins to flourish among men.

www.ingramcontent.com/pod-product-compliance
Lightning Source LLC
Chambersburg PA
CBHW070822100426
42813CB00003B/451